50 Things to Do
with a Penknife

IMPORTANT SAFETY NOTICE

Using a penknife to work with wood and other materials inherently includes the risk of injury and damage. We cannot guarantee that creating the projects in this book is safe for everyone. For this reason, this book is sold without warranties or guarantees of any kind, expressed or implied, and the publisher and the author disclaim any liability for injuries, losses or damages caused in any way by the content of this book or the reader's use of the tools needed to complete the projects presented herein. The publisher and the author urge readers to thoroughly review each project and to understand the use of all tools before beginning any project.

First published in the United Kingdom in 2017 by
Pavilion
43 Great Ormond Street
London
WC1N 3HZ

ISBN 978-1-911216-86-5

A CIP catalogue record for this book is available from the British Library.

10 9 8 7 6 5 4 3 2 1

Reproduction by Mission Productions Ltd, Hong Kong
Printed and bound by 1010 Printing International Ltd, China

This book can be ordered direct from the publisher at www.pavilionbooks.com

50 Things to Do with a Penknife

Matt Collins

Illustrated by Maria Nilsson

PAVILION

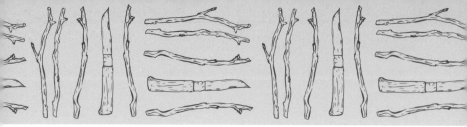

Contents

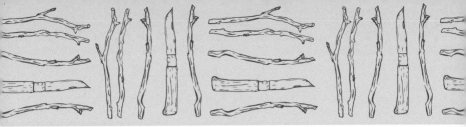

Introduction

Faced with that age-old hypothetical question, if you were marooned on a desert island and allowed one implement as a companion for utility and survival, what would you choose? An axe? A handsaw? Perhaps a box of matches, or even a length of robust rope? The top answer must surely be a penknife, as what other tool could be as dependable or versatile? Conceived as far back as the Iron Age, compact folding knives have proven to be indispensable personal possessions, taking on a wide range of forms over centuries of use. Whoever it is carried by and however it is used, this simple, lightweight device has become a popular resource for occupation and hobby alike.

With a hinged blade that may be stowed conveniently after use, penknives are as safe to operate as they are easy to maintain. Resilient, hard-wearing handles protect the blades from the elements, such as rust from water damage, as well as from blunting if dropped or knocked. Furthermore, being that much smaller when folded, the portability of a penknife is perhaps its signature feature, fitting neatly into a jacket pocket or toolbox compartment. Of course a penknife is not restricted exclusively to a blade and a handle; there are a great many additional concealable accessories, ranging from scissors to screwdriver, corkscrew to toothpick. However, the inward-folding blade is what defines a penknife's fundamental appeal, and the blade itself is what makes this tool so useful.

While convenience and versatility make a penknife suitably industrious for survival on a hypothetical desert island, they also make it the perfect instrument for a less extreme application. Carving, or 'whittling', is a wonderfully creative and enjoyable pursuit, transforming ordinary sections of wood into ornate or useful items. One of the best things about whittling is that it can be enjoyed at a range of levels and abilities. There are many projects that will require a certain amount of determination – softening the edges of a spinning top for example, or sculpting the curve of a decorative ring. However, some of the most practical items are also the simplest to carve, and a sense of achievement is readily bestowed upon the persevering whittler. This book is intended as an introductory guide to carving many of these functional and rudimentary items, as well as a handful of more challenging whittling projects.

This book isn't only about wood whittling. The seven chapters feature alternative carving materials, and find creative uses for old wine corks as well as some inventive re-imagining of fruit and vegetables. There are also useful tasks, such as the preparation of a freshly caught fish, producing grafted apple trees and multiplying favourite woody shrubs. Whatever the task, a penknife remains at the centre – its implementation demonstrated via a concise set of illustrated steps.

There is also a useful introductory section that offers helpful information for anyone starting out with a penknife, or whittling for the first time. Detailing topics such as selection of carving materials, how to maintain and sharpen a blade, as well as the choice of penknife itself, these pages are a reference guide for the 50 projects featured in this book. Safe operation of a penknife is discussed, illustrating a range of controlled carving techniques intended to lower the risks of handling a blade. However, it should be remembered that a penknife will remain a sharp, hazardous tool, and therefore should always be treated with extreme care and, when necessary, adult supervision.

The tools of a trade or traditional craft share a commonality in their relationship with their master. Much like a potter's wheel or sculptor's chisel, a penknife is personal to its owner, and the more it is used and worked with, the more familiar it will feel in the hand. This should also be said of the craft itself, and whittling, when practised, can make for an engaging and intuitive activity. Furthermore, working so closely with organic material offers a connection with the natural world that few hobbies can match. Above all, however, carving should be a fun and relaxing recreation, absorbing in its elemental simplicity.

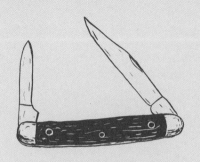

Selecting Your
Pocket Knife

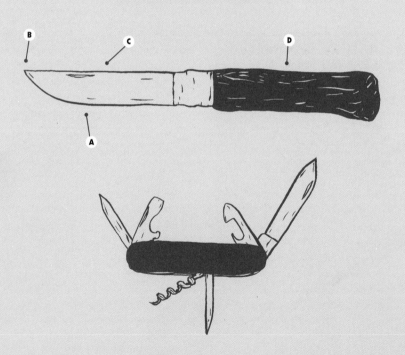

A pocket knife can come in many forms, ranging from a knife with a single, fixed blade, to a variety of multifunctional, foldaway Swiss Army-style knives. However, there is no rule dictating what a whittling knife should look like, and provided that your selected blade fulfils the basic functional criteria, the 'right' type of knife remains a personal choice. Your whittling knife may be one you're well acquainted with, and have put to use already, or it may have been a gift. Whatever the background, a suitable knife is one that is manoeuvrable, comfortable and, above all, sharp.

Not surprisingly, a good knife is a good blade. Carving material of any kind depends most crucially on a sharp blade (**A**). A dull or blunt edge not only inhibits the precision of each cut, but it also presents a danger to its handler. There's an old whittler's saying that goes, 'a dull knife is more dangerous than a sharp knife'. Of course a sharp knife is not a tool to be careless with, but the dangers are more obvious. A blunt knife offers its handler less control. There's a far greater chance of the knife slipping in the hand, due to the additional force that must be applied in order to make a cut. Therefore a sharp blade enables a more precise and controlled movement, improving the safety of any such operation.

A sharp blade should lead to a sharp tip (**B**), which is used to perform a number of whittling cuts, very often intricate and delicate ones. A sharp point is therefore critical to a suitable and versatile pocket knife. Many whittling cuts involve an exertion of pressure using the thumb or forefinger on top of the blade. It helps therefore to have a straight-topped blade (**C**), as opposed to a double-edged variety. And lastly, there is no substitute for a comfortable handle (**D**). If your knife does not sit smoothly and pleasantly in the hand, it will see far less use. This is often the unfortunate downfall of multifunctional, overly laden pocket knives, such as the Swiss Army knife.

Please note that in the UK it is illegal to carry a knife in public without good reason unless it is a knife with a folding blade 7.5cm (3in) long or less. Lock knives (that can be locked and refolded only by pressing a button) are not classified as folding knives.

More information on suppliers of knives, as well as other helpful kit, is detailed in Sources, page 143.

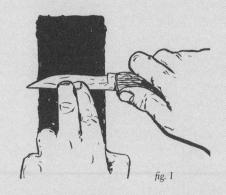

fig. 1

Maintaining Your Blade

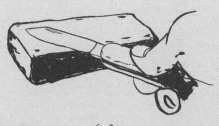

fig. 2

In case the point hasn't been made strongly enough already, a sharp edge really is the backbone of whittling. Each cut made using your pocket knife will result in the gradual dulling of its blade. Therefore it is necessary to keep a close check on the maintenance of the knife-edge to ensure that it is performing exactly as it should. The simplest (and most pocketable) sharpening tool is a 'whetstone'. Whetstones can be purchased from numerous high street outlets and online retailers. Ranging in size from 4–20cm (1½–8in), pocket knife whetstones are formed of two contrasting sides: a coarse, rough surface (for sharpening) and a smoother, finely graded surface (for 'finishing').

Sharpening

To sharpen your knife, either place the whetstone on a tabletop with the rough surface uppermost, or hold the stone in the palm of your hand with fingers and thumb kept below the top surface of the stone.

Lie your blade on the stone's rough surface, set at a 30-degree angle (see fig. 1). Draw the blade across the stone first on one side, then turn the blade over and repeat on the other side.

The knife-edge should be facing away when being drawn inwardly towards the handler. Repeat this action until the knife feels sharp; check by lightly running your thumb or fingers across the blade from left to right, taking care not to follow the line of the blade.

Finishing

Turning the whetstone over, use the smoother side in much the same way in order to provide a smooth finish (see fig. 2). Afterwards, wipe the knife using a damp or lightly oiled cloth.

Cleaning

When working with a folding knife, such as a penknife or Swiss Army knife, it is important also to maintain and clean the body of the knife. With frequent use, dust and debris often collects within the handle into which the blade is folded. If left unchecked, remnants like these can cause damage to the blade itself. Knives of this type require a light oiling from time to time in order to lubricate the folding mechanism. Regular 3-in-1 oil is a good choice for this purpose.

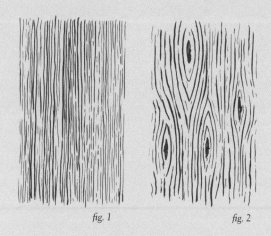

fig. 1   fig. 2

Selecting Your
Carving Material

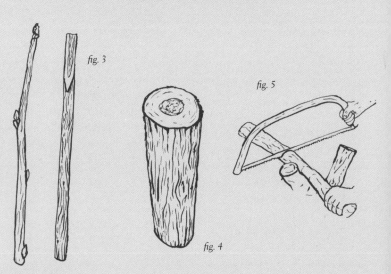

fig. 3

fig. 5

fig. 4

Although the items in this book are whittled from a handful of different materials, this page contains a little more information specific to working with wood.

Carving with wood

One of the wonderful things about trees is the great diversity in the qualities of their lumber. This is in fact one of the distinctions by which felled or harvested trees can be identified and told apart. Varying in many ways, from colour and grain to weight and texture, wood also differs between its 'green' (fresh or recently cut wood) and 'seasoned' (dried, hardened wood) stages. The wood of a growing alder tree (*Alnus* spp.), for example, is a pale, creamy colour. However, once split and exposed, alder wood quickly oxidizes, staining a deep orange hue that will dull slowly as it seasons.

Seasoning

This is the process by which cut wood is dried out. Once seasoned, wood will become tougher to carve and less pliable, and will tend to splinter more easily. Whittling with dry material like this certainly makes harder work for the knife, but perseverance will produce attractive results. Building up a little stock of seasoned wood can be a good idea – collecting off-cuts or fallen branches that can

be dried in a shed and later drawn upon for carving.

Although green wood is a much softer material to carve, it can be less sturdy to work with and, in the case of a few trees, can contain sticky sap that makes whittling an unpleasant and difficult task. Therefore the ideal carving wood tends to be somewhere in between: neither fresh from the tree nor fully seasoned.

The natural moisture content of a tree species is another factor affecting its carving suitability. Being a damp-tolerant, riverside tree, willow has a naturally high moisture content, as does alder, poplar and sycamore. Material taken from these trees tends to be softer to work with than that of beech, hornbeam and oak, all of which are suited to less saturated soils and produce a heavier wood.

Grain

This is a word commonly associated with carving and woodwork more generally. A more comprehensive understanding of grain is necessary when working with sawn or milled timber. Put simply, however, 'grain' is the general term used to describe the pattern of fibres that run through wood. The density of these fibres determines whether a wood has a 'coarse' or 'fine' grain, while their direction impacts upon the 'straightness' of a grain. The straighter the grain, the easier a wood is to work with, as the fibres run in a clear and linear direction (see fig. 1, straight grain, and fig. 2, curvy grain). Wood of this nature will therefore also cleave more evenly when split. But the main rule to remember is always to carve *with* the direction of the grain, rather than against it. The latter will cause the fibres to tear, resulting in untidy fragmented strokes.

Hardwoods vs softwoods

There is much discussion surrounding the type of trees best suited for carving, but the terms 'hardwood' and 'softwood' are not to be confused with 'broadleaf' and 'coniferous'. Broadleaf trees are often referred to as hardwoods. However, hardwood trees can produce both hard and soft wood material – species of lime tree (*Tilia* spp.), for example, yield a soft, malleable lumber (known as 'basswood'), whereas oak wood (*Quercus* spp.) is heavy and tough. Coniferous trees are typically known as softwoods, and include cedar, fir and pine. Due to their particularly straight grain, these conifers are among the favourites for carving, but pine in its green state should be avoided on account of its gum-like sap.

Pith

Pith is the spongy material found at the centre of a young stem. Slicing a twig diagonally will reveal the extent of its pith (see fig. 3). The diameter of pith will vary from one tree species to another, and you're likely to encounter it when whittling with thin, young, twiggy material. In dry or seasoned wood, hardened pith can be tougher and a little more amenable to carving (see fig. 4). However, it is best to avoid using stems with a particularly large pith in general.

Notes

Many of the 50 projects in this book begin with a stick or length of wood that has been selected to suit the task in hand. Neither a hardwood nor softwood is stipulated unless necessary. In addition, these lengths of wood have been prepared in advance of the 'steps' by being sawn flat at the ends (see fig. 5). To avoid repetition, this part of the whittling process has been omitted from the steps in some of the items.

Please ensure that your carving material is acquired responsibly; collect only as much as you'll need and check that purchased timber has been sustainably sourced.

Carving Techniques

When it comes to whittling, techniques tend to vary from person to person. Safety is the key element to consider however, and is perhaps the overriding factor dictating the composition of each cutting stroke. The following examples, each featuring important safety tips, demonstrate a series of fairly basic cutting techniques. The illustrations relate to carving with wood, but most can be applied to the other materials used in this book, be they cork, carrot or cucumber.

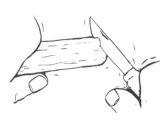

Stop cut

The stop cut is perhaps the simplest of the strokes and covers a multitude of actions. Essentially it is an exertion of downward force on the blade in order to indent or mark your material, and is typically used to create an initial guiding imprint or a point to which you can subsequently carve. It is advisable to place your whittling project on a hard surface before making a stop cut to add stability.

Paring cut

This is the traditional cut used for cutting an apple: with the apple in one hand, the knife handle is gripped firmly in the other. Using the thumb of your knifed hand to steady the action, draw the blade inwards towards the thumb. The stroke itself encourages a swivelling motion in the wrist, lifting the blade as it travels, and delivering a smooth and shallow cut. The safest way to make a cut like this is to tuck both the fingers and thumb out of the way, ideally underneath the whittled object. You can also wear a protective glove or thumb guard.

Push cut

This is an invaluable technique when it comes to carving with accuracy, allowing the whittler to achieve delicate and ornate results. By using the thumb of your un-knifed hand to exert force on the blade, a steady cut can be made, be it long or short in length. This carving technique is also particularly safe as it offers maximum control, with the blade aimed away from the body. Use a push cut to round off edges and carve notches into wood.

Pull cut

With the penknife held in position, use your other hand to administer the cut by drawing your whittled object towards the blade. Again, this is a safer form of cutting technique, keeping the blade pointing outwards and locked in a fixed position.

Split cut

This cut is used to split, cleave or 'rive' a straight-grained piece of wood. Stand a stick or straight branch on a flat surface with your blade placed at its centre. Using a piece of heavy wood, knock the knife downwards.

Helpful Extras

One of the joys of whittling is its rudimental simplicity. As the world becomes familiar with increasingly complicated and elaborate apparatus, be it for work, entertainment or practicality, there's something remarkably satisfying in working with a penknife and wood. For the most part, the 50 carving projects in this book involve only these two basic components, but occasionally a project will call for one or more items from the following list. Although not all vital necessities, access to a good saw (see page 18), as well as a few sandpaper options, will prove immensely useful in the undertaking of any carving project. More information on suppliers of the tools listed can be found in Sources, page 143.

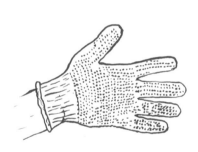
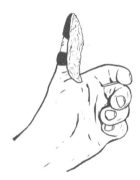

Safety

There are many precautions that can be taken to reduce the risks of carving with a sharp knife. Performing even the most basic of whittling strokes can present the potential for a hazardous incident. Therefore you may wish to purchase a pair of cut-resistant gloves or a simple thumb guard. Whittling gloves are typically lined with steel thread and fibreglass, offering protection for your hands without majorly affecting their dexterity. A thumb guard will be less comprehensively protective, but it will prove enormously useful when making delicate paring cuts.

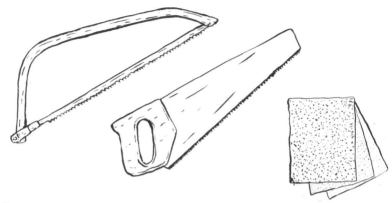

Saws

Whether you're taking a branch from a tree or cutting larger pieces of wood to size, a bow saw (above left) will make light work of the task in hand. With its deeply toothed, free-strung blade, this type of saw is designed for cutting green wood quickly and easily. When sawing smaller diameter wood, or making neater, more precise cuts, a wood saw (above centre) is a preferable tool to use. Although there is a variety of wood saws available, a fine-toothed blade is particularly useful for this sort of task, cutting cleanly and with increased accuracy.

Sandpaper

While the merits of sanding are obvious, it is also worth noting that not all wood carvings need conclude with the application of sandpaper. Sanding will certainly smooth the pares and cuts made while sculpting, but it will also disguise them, removing character from what is ultimately a homemade and personal craft. That said, sandpaper is generally an indispensable component of the whittler's kit, however often it's employed.

Sandpaper is graded according to 'grit' size. This relates to the size of the abrasive fragments glued to the paper itself: larger grit for sanding rougher surfaces, smaller grit for sanding a finer finish. Although there is a vast range of grit sizes, the ones referred to in this book are: 'coarse' (40–50 grit), 'medium' (60–80 grit) and 'fine' (100–120 grit).

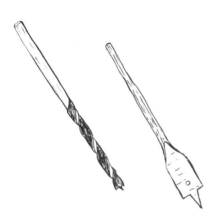

In the absence of sandpaper, particularly if you're out and about, stones displaying a coarse surface can make for a helpful, foraged alternative.

Drill and bits

Drill bits are helpful implements to have handy, whether used in partnership with a drill or as tools in their own right. While their sharp point can be used to indent or mark a sculpture, they're also, let's face it, much quicker at making precise holes than a knife, particularly when carving out a substantial section of wood. A selection of bit sizes is ideal, including some of the larger, flat-headed variety.

Clamp and oil

Occasionally the use of a small G- or C-clamp can make certain carving actions a little easier to tackle. None of the projects in this book depends on the use of a clamp, but they can be useful.

As outlined in Maintaining your blade, page 10, a periodic application of oil helps to prolong the life of a penknife and keep it in good working order. Any high-quality, multipurpose oil will do the trick, applied lightly to the hinge and blade. Applying finishing oil, such as boiled linseed, Danish or teak oil, can be a nice way to round off whittling projects made using dry, seasoned wood. Not only does the oil enrich the carving's appearance, but it also helps to preserve the wood itself. Finishing oil should be applied sparingly at first, allowing time for it to dry before adding a second or third coat.

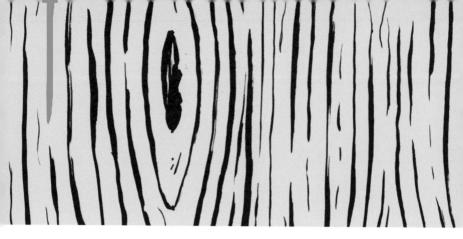

Quick Things

Included here are a few quick items to get started with.
Incorporating the whittling strokes outlined in Carving
Techniques (pages 15–16), these projects provide the
chance to familiarize yourself with the safe operation of a
knife. Mastering these strokes will allow future projects to be
undertaken with relative ease, applying careful and effective
cuts within a controlled and safe approach.

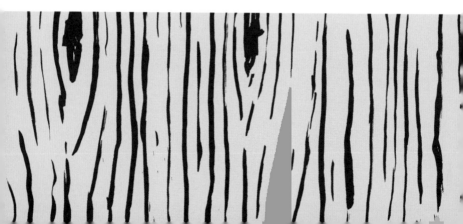

1

Sharpen a pencil

Sharpening a pencil may at first seem like the most basic of penknife applications. However, maintaining a fine tip requires a little more precision than is often considered, and provides an excellent example of a controlled push cut. Although it may be tempting to use quick, driving stokes, heavy cuts like these often result in the pencil being whittled, quite literally, into oblivion. Switching to the push cut will ensure that you get the maximum life from your lead.

1. Holding the pencil firmly in one hand, use your thumb to push your penknife blade, angled slightly downwards in the other hand. Repeat this action all the way round, revealing fresh lead at the tip.

2. While maintaining a firm grip on the pencil, use a finer push cut to whittle the lead tip itself into a sharp point.

2

Doorstop

There's nothing more aggravating than watching a door slowly closing after you've set it open. But while doorstops are inexpensive, they're also simple to carve. You may find that a wooden doorstop will perform better than the usual plastic alternative too, creating more friction with which to steady a heavy door. Whittling the sloping face of a rustic, wooden doorstop is also a great way to get to grips with another important carving stroke: the pull cut. With a length of wood drawn firmly in towards your knife using one hand, the blade will cut smoothly, held tightly in the other hand.

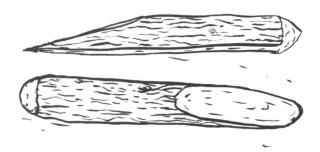

1. Using short push cuts, whittle off the edges from one end of a straight stick of about 10cm (4in) in length. Make sure that your forefinger is tucked safely away from the direction of the cut.

2. Whittle this same end into a soft, rounded point by further shortening the length of your cuts.

3. Create a flat surface on one of the sides by shaving towards you using a paring cut. Angle the blade slightly upwards to avoid it cutting too deeply, and keep fingers tucked in low, away from the path of the blade.

4. Turning the wood over, cut a slope at the opposite end from the rounded point, using a pull cut. This will create the slope that goes under the door. Do this by holding the knife still and pulling the wood towards you. Repeat this pull cut until the slope is finished.

3

Flowerbed marker

Indicating where, or which, seeds have been sown in the garden is a necessary task, particularly if they are liable to be disturbed before they have had a chance to germinate. Flowerbed markers tend to serve a temporary purpose however, and consequentially the use of plastic labelling can become expensive unless regularly reused. Plastic markers also have an annoying habit of turning up in the compost heap or being left in the soil, jarring with the natural environment even at the best of times. Making your own wooden markers offers an inexpensive and rustic alternative that, if left or lost, will ultimately compost and return naturally to the soil.

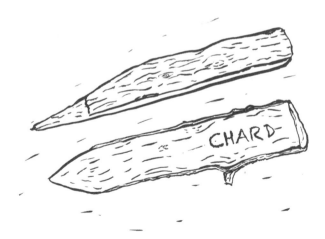

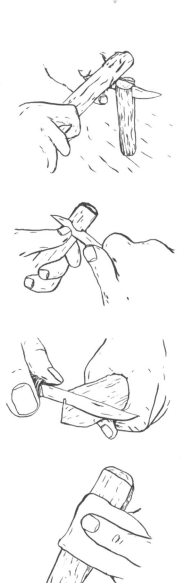

1. Find a straight and relatively dry piece of wood and cut it to approximately 15cm (6in) in length. Use a split cut to split it down the middle.

2. Take one half of the split wood. Whittle one end of the rounded side to a slope, using pull cuts in a similar way to the Doorstop on page 22.

3. Using similar pull cuts, taper in the sides of the slope to form a sharp point.

4. Use a medium-grit sandpaper to smooth the flat side of the marker so that it can be written on with a marker pen.

4

Bookmark

The distinctive grain running through different kinds of wood is an inherently attractive feature, displaying the unique fingerprint of a given branch or tree. As wood is split open these curves and circles are exposed, offering an ornamental quality to 'riven' (made from split wood) objects like this simple bookmark. Softwoods like cedar and fir are a good choice of source material for this project as their straight grain will split more smoothly and evenly than many of the harder woods. Working with partially dry material is also recommended, as the sap in green softwood can be sticky and therefore somewhat troublesome to work with.

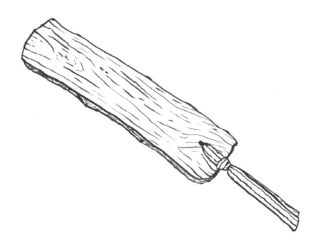

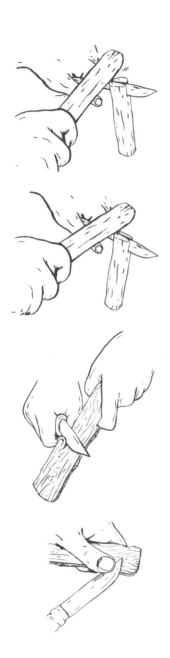

1. Taking a straight piece of wood roughly 10–15cm (4–6in) in length, split it in half using a split cut. Make the cut just off the centre of the wood.

2. Taking one of the two split pieces, place your penknife 0.5cm (¼in) back from the last cut and repeat the same cut.

3. Clean up both faces of your split wood by scraping the blade of your penknife gently downwards along the grain. Further smoothing of the surface can be achieved using a medium-grit sandpaper.

4. Round the edges of the bookmark with a series of careful push cuts. A hole can then be made using either a drill or the tip of your knife, so that string or ribbon may be tied to it to complete the bookmark.

5

Letter opener

Here's a quick task useful for practising some short, fine carving strokes. Getting to grips with controlled cuts like these will allow you to add ornament to an object, demonstrated here with the shaping of a letter opener from a wooden popsicle stick. Ice-lolly sticks tend to be produced from birch, one of the softer hardwood trees, making for an excellent carving material. It is still important to make sure that your knife remains sharp throughout the process however, returning it to the whetstone if necessary to maintain that crucial sharp blade.

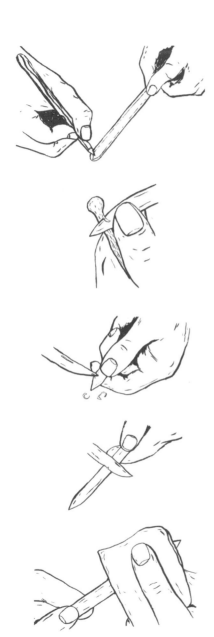

1. Draw the outline of a sword onto an ice-lolly stick, curving in at the edges before the handle.

2. Using both push and paring strokes, carefully cut away the sword shape with your penknife.

3. Whittle a sharp tip (like that of a pencil) at the pointed end.

4. Whittle the ice-lolly stick edges to a slope, beginning at the handle of the sword and cutting down towards the point.

5. Sand your letter opener using a fine-grit sandpaper to finish.

6

Gift box book

Many a great tale has been told of the book-smuggle, whereby precious items are sneaked into secure places, cunningly hidden within the pages of a book. Whether it was taking a hammer into a prison or jewellery through customs, this clandestine operation has become the stuff of legends. This undertaking can also make for a fun gesture or gift, concealing a token for a comrade or present for a friend. Do make sure that you have consent however, before permanently damaging the contents of a book.

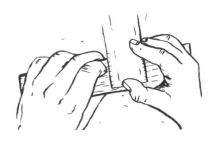

1. Measure the depth of your gift and choose a book that will be dense enough to conceal it by squeezing the pages together in one hand, and measuring the thickness at the centre of the book. This will ensure that there are enough uncut pages at the beginning and end to hide those that will be cut. Using the nail of your forefinger, open the page at the top of the marked depth. This is where you will need to start cutting.

2. Place the gift on the opened page and trace a rectangle around it with a pencil. Place a sheet of stiff board below the last page that you will be cutting out. This will stop your cut short, so that you won't slice into more pages than necessary.

3. Sharpen your knife! Using careful stop cuts, slice down along the traced lines and remove cuttings. You will need to do this in stages, cutting through 5–10 pages at a time until you reach the bottom.

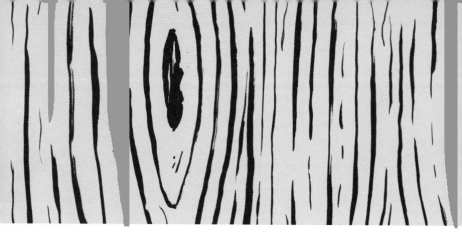

Into the Woods

While most modern-day camping apparatus fits neatly into a rucksack, there are many items that can be assembled on-site, using materials found around the camp itself. Whether you're in need of a spoon for the pot or a peg for hanging wet clothes, this chapter provides a helpful guide to carving some of those all-important implements for a trip into the great outdoors. Do think sustainably when collecting your wood, seeking out fallen branches and sticks before sourcing carving material from living trees. Also avoid using poisonous woods when whittling culinary utensils.

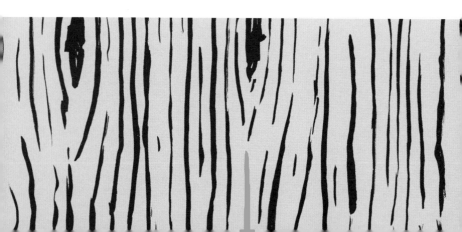

7

Willow whistle

Sculpting a whistle from the green and lithe stems of a springtime willow is a carving tradition passed down through generations of keen whittlers. As the sap rises and flows through young willow branches during the early summer months, their bark is particularly supple, and subsequently easy to separate from the stem. Because of this, willow is the ideal source material for this satisfying carving project, offering a malleable texture that may be sculpted with relative ease. As with many whittling exercises, this one can take a few tries to master, but the result will be noteworthy, and persistence is the key.

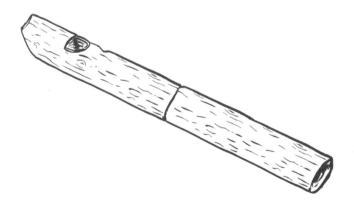

1. For this exercise you'll need a straight stem of green willow, roughly 1.5–2cm (⅝–¾in) in diameter and 20–30cm (8–12in) in length. Using a pull cut, create a shallow slope at one end of the stick.

2. With the slope facing away from you, place the blade of your penknife 3cm (1¼in) back from the beginning of the slope cut, and make a stop cut.

4. You now need to remove the bark without breaking it. Placing your penknife blade roughly 10cm (4in) back from the slope, make a circular cut around the stick as deep as the bark. This is best achieved by holding the knife in a fixed position and turning the stick with your other hand.

3. With your knife 1cm (⅜in) back from the stop cut made in step 2, push cut downwards towards it, carving out a thin wedge.

5. Loosen the bark by placing it on your knee and tapping with the handle of your penknife. Turn the stick in your other hand while you tap, forcing the bark to come away evenly from the stem inside. Take your time with this – you should be able to feel when the bark is ready to be pulled off.

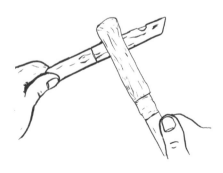

6. Carefully pull the bark from the stick and place it to one side.

7. Taking the bare wood, place your knife inside the groove, against the stop cut made in step 2. Use a push cut to remove the top of the stick, creating a flat surface.

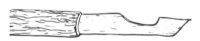

8. Repeat steps 2 and 3, making a slightly deeper stop cut this time, and push cutting towards it from 2cm (¾in) back, rather than 1cm (⅜in).

9. The side profile of your willow stick should now look like this.

10. Taking the bark section that was removed in step 6, carefully slide it back in place, lining up the bark hole with the whistle hole. Blow through; it should whistle! If not, you may need to check that the flat surface made in step 7 is flat enough and is letting enough air through.

8

Tent peg

Tent pegs forever remain the bane of the camping trip.
Traditional metal pegs far too often bend under pressure,
and are the first things to go missing after a weekend
under canvas. Here's a quick and easy method of knocking
up your very own pegs using material close to hand.
Little wooden pegs make for even more reliable fixings
for a tent of any size, and you can have peace of mind
in knowing that any left behind will decompose naturally
back into the surroundings from which they came.

1. Taking a branch of roughly 15cm (6in) length and 2–3cm (¾–1¼in) thickness, round off the top using a downwards cut. This will help prolong the life of the peg and set apart the top from the bottom.

2. Using the top end of your blade nearest the handle, mark out a line, 4cm (1½in) down from the top of the peg. Press down firmly and roll the blade to achieve a clear indentation.

3. Cut downwards towards the line from 1cm (⅜in) back. Remove the shaving.

4. Repeat this cutting action until a notch shape begins to develop.

5. Shave the opposite end of the peg into a tip. This will be the end driven into the ground – it needn't be too sharp.

9

Spoon

There is perhaps no single object more closely associated with carving than the spoon. Whether it's the roughly cut, functional kind, or a more delicate, ornamental example, fashioning a spoon from a single piece of wood remains one of the whittler's favourite pursuits. There are many approaches to handcrafting a spoon, and indeed many tools. Use of a 'hook knife' for example, with its rounded blade, will achieve a far more precise curve than a straight blade. However, if it's a rudimentary, hardworking spoon that you're after, a penknife is just the tool for the job.

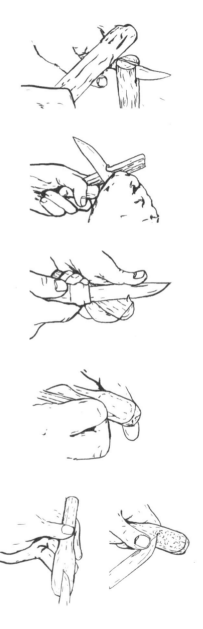

1. Split a 15–20cm (6–8in) length of round wood using a split cut.

2. Taking one of the split pieces, pare down one end from roughly near the middle, shaping it into the spoon's handle.

3. Turning the wood around to work on the spoon end, shave off the corners using a push cut. The basic outline of a spoon should now be taking shape. Using a pencil, draw a circle at the spoon end. This will indicate the area to be whittled out to indent the spoon. To begin the indentation, make a stop cut in the centre of the circle using the top of your penknife. Firmly twist the knife to cut out a small circular wedge.

4. Beginning at the circular indent, use small paring cuts to slowly etch away the inside of the spoon. Take your time as the first few cuts will be the trickiest. With the spoon now taking shape, finish and round off the handle end with a few more strokes. Once you're finished, use medium-grit sandpaper to smooth the inside of the spoon as well as the handle shaft.

10

Feather stick

There's no smoke without fire, as they say, but damp wood will often produce a good deal more of one than the other. If your campfire tinder is wet or even soaked from rain, lighting a roaring blaze can become a near impossible task. The feather stick is a fantastic solution to this infuriating problem. While the outer surface of fallen sticks and branches may be sodden, there is often a good source of dry wood at the centre, and with a few simple cuts, these dry centres can be converted into nature's own firelighters. Once you've finished carving, begin your fire by setting light to the whittled shavings of the feather stick, before adding larger wood to the flames.

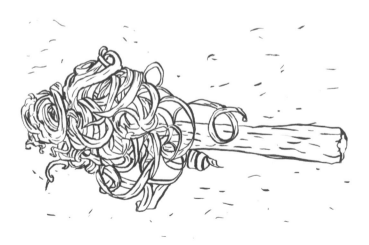

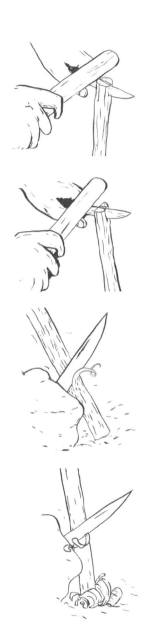

1. Taking a fallen branch or length of wood, split it down the middle using a split cut.

2. Split the wood again into quarters, using the same technique. The inner wood will usually be significantly drier than the exterior bark.

3. To begin the feathering process, place a split quarter of wood upright on a firm surface and make a downwards cut from halfway along its length to just above the bottom. As you're doing so, tilt the blade of your penknife upwards. This will result in a shallow cut while also creating 'ridges' at either side of the cut.

4. Choose one of the ridges and cut downwards along it, keeping the blade tilted upwards while forcing it down along the stick, stopping 2.5cm (1in) or so from the bottom. Repeat this cut, whittling each ridge as you work your way around the bottom half of the wood. You can create more 'feathers' by cutting behind the first strokes, using the same starting point halfway up the wood.

11

Fish hook

Nothing epitomizes a riverside camping trip better than freshly caught fish cooking over an open fire. Along with a little bait and line, a homemade fish hook can provide all you'll need to secure that campfire feast. The following steps demonstrate how to convert a forked twig into a tough and sharp hook, requiring nothing more than the trees around you and your trusty pocket knife. When fishing, hooks are occasionally lost or snagged under stones. While metal hooks will remain and become harmful to the environment, your wooden tackle will ultimately decompose.

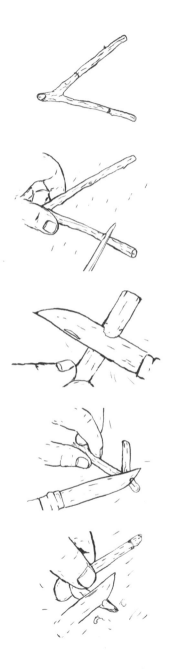

1. Select a forked twig, 0.5cm (¼in) in diameter. Measuring from the fork in the wood, mark 4cm (1½in) on one of the forked stems and 2cm (¾in) on the other. The longer stem will become the main shaft and the shorter stem will make the hook.

2. Use angled stop cuts to split off the excess sections of twig.

3. Remove the bark and make a groove at the top of the main shaft all the way around.

4. Remove the excess of twig below the fork in the wood, and round it off using a series of small push cuts.

5. Give your hook a sharp point by carefully whittling down the end of the hook point.

12

Slingshot

Almost anyone with a love of the outdoors will, at some
point, have had a go at making a slingshot. Ranging from
the simplicity of a rubber band strung between the fingers,
to the traditional carved catapult shown in this project,
slingshots are an enjoyable way to launch small objects over
large distances. The steps shown here demonstrate how to
whittle a forked branch into the body of a slingshot, fashioning
its projection from elastic, and a casting pouch from an old belt.
A good source of elastic can be foraged from a second-hand
bicycle tyre, cutting a thin strip out of the inner tubing.
While slingshots may be fun to make, they can be a dangerous
device and should be used responsibly. Stones and other heavy
or sharp objects should never be used as firing material, nor
should slingshots ever be fired at humans or animals.

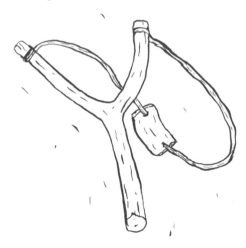

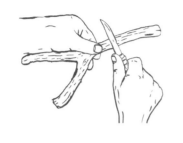

1. Select a thick 'Y'-shaped stick (this can be cut from a branch or found on the ground and trimmed). The stick needs to be solid and not brittle, making seasoned wood the best choice. Shave off the bark using your penknife.

2. Score a line around each of the fork tops, 1cm (⅜in) down from the tips.

3. Cut upwards into the marked lines using a push cut. Cut downwards the other way to create a notch. Repeat this action on both lengths of the fork, all the way around, forming deep notches. These will hold the elastic in step 4. Sand the wood smooth when finished.

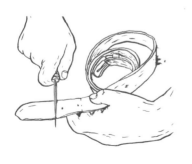

4. For the central pouch pictured in the main image, cut a section from an old, unused belt that includes two buckle holes (check with the owner first). Thread a tough, thick length of elastic through the belt holes and tie the ends around the notches in the fork. The belt section should sit at the centre of the elastic.

13

Fork

Among the kitchen utensils well suited for quick carving, a fork is probably the most useful. If you're camping in the great outdoors and require that all-important implement, follow these easy steps to carve yourself a wooden solution. In the time it takes for your campfire to roar, you'll have a fork ready and waiting, whittled from the material around you and fit for any fireside feast. When carving an item to eat with, it is wise to be certain of the wood you're using, and to be sure that you're not carving with a poisonous species.

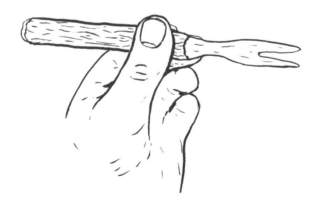

1. Select a 1.5–2cm ($\frac{5}{8}$–$\frac{3}{4}$in) diameter stem of wood between 15 and 20cm (6–8in) in length. Round it off at one end using short push cuts.

2. At the other end, taper one side by running the blade flatly downwards from 3cm (1¼in) back. Do this on the other side as well, creating a wedge shape.

3. Your stick should now look something like this.

4. Using a pen or the tip of your knife, mark a 'V' shape on one of the sloping surfaces of the tapered end. This indicates where the fork prongs will be.

5. Cut around the 'V' with short, careful strokes. You may wish to wear a safety glove on your non-knifed hand.

6. Use push cuts to define the prongs further, including the slope down to the tips.

7. Push cut towards the pronged end from 5cm (2in) back along the handle but stop halfway. Using a paring cut, cut down towards the previous cut – this will create an indent before the point where the prong head begins.

8. Repeat step 7, indenting all the way around the wood.

9. Make closer cuts to further refine the indent, before sanding to finish.

14

Spatula

A spatula is a utensil of modest design yet irreplaceable function, and is especially handy for those alfresco meals cooked on a campfire. Here's a useful technique for whittling a rough and ready spatula from a short length of wood. Green wood will suit this exercise well, but be sure to choose a suitable, non-toxic species to carve with, as your spatula will be used in the preparation of food. Always make sure that you are certain of a wood's properties and origin before it is used for cooking.

1. Look for a small, straight log and split it in two, placing your penknife blade just off the centre.

2. Draw the outline of your spatula on the flat surface of one of the split halves, using a pen or pencil.

3. Standing the split half upright, make a second split cut 1cm (⅜in) or so behind the first, cutting out a thin wedge.

4. Carve out the handle with a series of careful cuts.

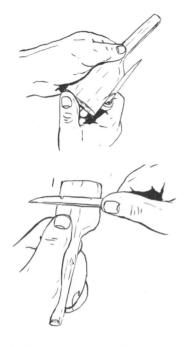

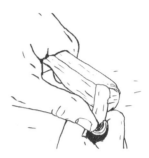

6. At this point, decide which surface will be the top and which will be the bottom. Carve a slope at the end of the spatula, from bottom to top.

5. Carve out the spatula head shape, and even the flat surfaces by drawing your blade across them.

7. Taper the entire bottom surface slightly so that the head of the spatula narrows towards the end.

8. Use the back of your blade to rub down and smooth the spatula surfaces all around. If your penknife is of the kind with a locking system, you should engage it to prevent the blade from closing back into the knife handle.

15

Clothes peg

The clothes peg is a useful item around the house but it becomes even more handy when you're out in the woods. Whether you want to dry clothes on a line, or fasten canvas to a wire, an adaptable peg becomes a valuable tool. Clothes pegs needn't be added to the essential equipment list however, as they can be easily fashioned with your trusty penknife and foraged material from the woods around you. The example here uses an elastic band to bind the split wood, but a strip of bicycle inner tube would work equally well, tied in a knot to keep it tight.

1. Split an 8–10cm (3¼–4in) length of wood down the middle using a split cut.

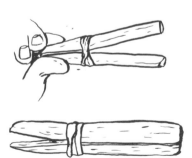

2. Taking one of the split halves, place your penknife about 3cm (1¼in) from the end.

3. Cut downwards, tapering the wood. Repeat this action until the taper is complete. Repeat the same action with the other split half.

4. Place the split ends back together and tie them together with a small elastic band, just before the point at which the ends begin to taper.

16

Walking stick

The hand-carved walking stick is often a whittler's signature object. Embracing the natural quirks and features of an individual branch or stem, fashioning these sticks depends on the wood selection as much as the carving itself. Although typically cut from coppiced hazel or ash trees, there is no rule dictating the type of wood that can be used, and the choice is entirely personal. The carving process outlined in this project makes use of branching material, incorporating one arm of a forked stick as a handle. However, a simpler version can be fashioned from a straight piece of wood. Once completed, walking sticks like these can be embellished further by adding ornate patterns or decorative carved illustration.

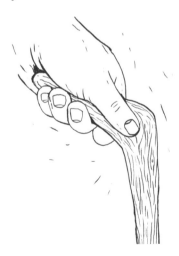

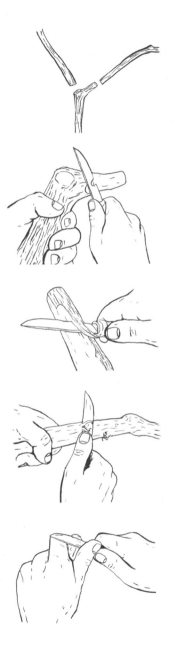

1. Select an appropriate, strong branch and prepare it with a saw. Remove the side shoots, leaving the handle shape at the top and a good length of straight stick at the bottom.

2. Trim off any little side shoots using your knife, and begin to shape and smooth the handle, removing the bark as you carve. Approach any knots in the wood with care, flattening them down slowly with short, shallow cuts.

3. Whittle down the main stick shaft, removing the bark until you get to the smooth heartwood underneath. You can use long strokes as the bark should come away relatively easily.

4. Rub the back of your blade down the stick to smooth the wood. Repeat the same action for the handle. If your penknife is of the kind with a locking system, you should engage it to prevent the blade from closing back into the knife handle.

5. Round the end of the handle using short push cuts. Do the same with the base of the stick.

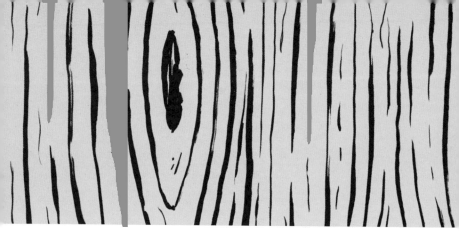

Around the House

Whether it's a practical household addition or a decorative
alternative to an everyday staple, the next set of projects will
put your knife to good use in the home. Items in this chapter
can also make wonderful gifts, such as crochet hooks,
hairpins and the surprisingly handy page holder. Whittled
gifts like these offer a bespoke, handcrafted present,
personalized for their recipient.

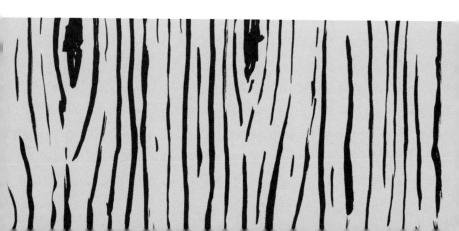

17

Crochet hook

While shop-bought crochet hooks won't break the bank, it can be nice to make your own, personalizing them to your own requirements in length and diameter. Best carved from a lightweight hardwood such as birch or hazel, these homemade hooks offer a rustic charm that befits this popular needlecraft. Wooden crochet hooks are best carved using dry material, as this will allow you to sand the wood down to a fine finish, ensuring that it doesn't snag on the yarn.

1. Cut a 20cm (8in) stem of roughly pencil thickness. Use pull cuts to remove the bark at one end.

2. Round the very top of the bare end using small push cuts.

3. Use a stop cut to carefully mark a line 0.5cm (¼in) down from the rounded end. Now make a cut in the same place, but this time cut slightly towards the end at a downwards angle. This will begin the shape of the hook. See next step for further illustration.

4. Using careful push cuts, cut up towards the line from 1.5cm (⅝in) back, forming an indent.

5. Repeat steps 3 and 4 until the head of the crochet hook begins to look like this. Sand it thoroughly afterwards using a medium-grit sandpaper.

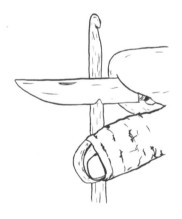

6. To make the thumb rest for your crochet hook, measure 5–6cm (2–2½in) down from the head and pare downwards by 1cm (⅜in). You may wish to wear a thumb guard or glove for protection while making the cuts for the thumb rest.

7. Pare or push a similar cut from the other direction, and repeat until a hollow or indent is made. Sand the indent to finish, making it as smooth as the rest of the hook.

18

Chopsticks

Carving chopsticks is a great way to make use of off-cuts of wood that might otherwise go to waste. Provided the grain runs straight and is free from knots, these simple utensils can be whittled as easily using seasoned wood as they can be with green. If you are carving with green wood however, do make sure that the wood you choose is toxin-free and is safe to eat with. Yew, for example, should be avoided as all parts, including the wood, are poisonous to humans. If you are unsure about a particular wood's toxicity properties, it is best to seek an alternative carving material.

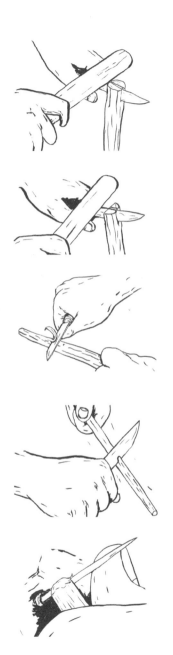

1. Split a straight section of wood down the middle. Choose a piece somewhere between 20 and 30cm (8–12in), and 2–3cm (¾–1¼in) in diameter.

2. Take one of the split halves and cleave it again.

3. Take one of the split quarters of wood. Use careful pull strokes to taper it down from one end. Turn the stick after each stroke, so the taper is even all round. Keep stopping and looking to check that it is straight and is not being cut at an angle.

4. Continue to whittle the stick down, applying shorter, finer strokes to avoid cutting away too much material.

5. Carve a rounded edge at the thicker end using short push cuts.

19

Button

Here's a great way to craft a simple yet practical button from a fallen branch or stick. The basic design is outlined here, but you can experiment further with your buttons, refining the shape and size to fit a range of different applications. Whether you're in need of a last-minute replacement or seeking a more 'natural look' for your attire, get started with this whittled accessory, fresh from the great outdoors.

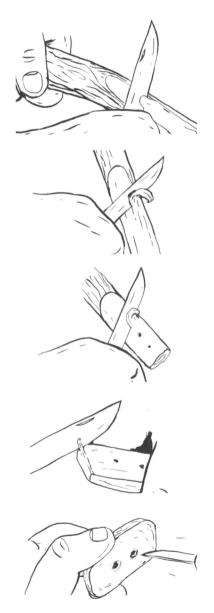

1. Taking a medium-sized branch or stick, use long pull cuts to create a flat surface roughly 4–5cm (1½–2in) in length.

2. Repeat the same action on the other side, creating a flat, rectangular shape at the bottom of your stick.

3. Drill two holes using either a drill or a spiked implement on your pocket knife if you have one, and whittle down the flat surfaces to make the rectangle a little sleeker and smoother.

4. Round the bottom two corners using short push cuts.

5. Sever the button from the stick using a wood saw. Alternatively you can use pull cuts to slowly whittle down the excess wood before snapping it cleanly away. Once the button is severed, repeat step 4 to round the opposite two corners and refine the shape, smoothing the edges all around and widening the holes with the tip of your knife.

20

Curtain rings

Whittling rings for your curtains may not be the quickest of carving exercises, but the results can be surprisingly attractive. Once you've mastered the first one, you'll soon find carving rings to be a leisurely and even therapeutic undertaking, replacing machined versions with a bespoke and original alternative. If you're setting up curtains from scratch, why not go one step further and fashion the rail too. Removing the bark with your penknife, a straight branch or stem from a young ash or hawthorn tree will make for the ideal cross piece on which to hang your rings.

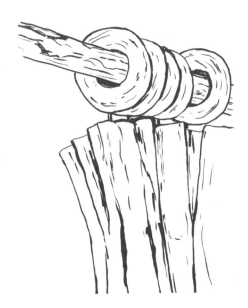

1. To make your rings you'll need a length of wood of a decent girth, ideally somewhere around 6–7cm (2½–2¾in). Saw the wood into manageable sections of up to 10cm (4in) in length, alleviating bends if your wood has a curve.

2. Take one of your sections of wood. Using a power drill and large-diameter bit (e.g. 2–3cm/¾–1¼in width), drill a hole down through the centre of the wood, stopping before the bit reaches the bottom. Use a vice to hold the wood to prevent it from slipping while you drill.

3. Mark a 1cm (⅜in) depth on the length of wood and saw it off. Repeat this step so that you end up with a number of rings.

4. Taking one of the rings, carve both the outer and middle edges to give them a rounded appearance.

5. With a series of closer cuts, round the ring edges further. Using a medium-grit sandpaper, spend some time sanding the wooden ring, evening out the cuts so that the round shape is smooth and regular.

6. Apply a coat of linseed oil and leave to dry. Add an eye screw (the type used for hanging picture frames) by either screwing it into the ring directly by hand, or drilling a very small pilot hole and then screwing it in. Your curtain ring is now ready for use. Repeat steps 4–6 to make more rings, taking further sections from step 1 when you require more carving material.

21

Ring holder

Handcrafting wooden ring holders makes for an enjoyable penknife project, working with a range of cutting strokes from rough to more delicate, finer carving. There's something very satisfying in whittling the perfect cone, the practice of which will become extremely useful for future wood carving ventures. Ring holders are best carved with dry, seasoned wood; different types of tree will offer different ornamental qualities, so it's worth experimenting. Watch out for overly knotted wood however, as knots will prove difficult to whittle smooth.

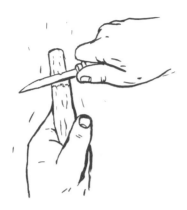

1. For this exercise you'll need a round, 10–15cm (4–6in) length of seasoned wood, 2–3cm (¾–1¼in) in diameter. Using long pull cuts from 5cm (2in) back, begin to taper one end.

2. With a pencil, lightly mark one side of the tapered end. This will be the side that is left relatively straight, while all other sides are whittled further, giving the cone a slight backwards lean that presents the ring better than if the cone was perfectly round.

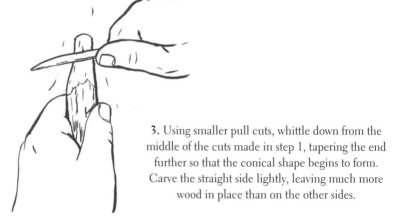

3. Using smaller pull cuts, whittle down from the middle of the cuts made in step 1, tapering the end further so that the conical shape begins to form. Carve the straight side lightly, leaving much more wood in place than on the other sides.

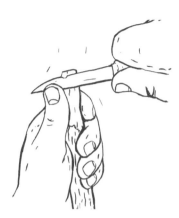

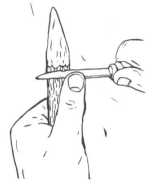

4. Whittle the very tip of the wood into a point with short push cuts. Avoid making it unnecessarily sharp.

5. Now use push cuts to shape the cone further. Once you've achieved a rough leaning cone, sand it down using a medium or coarse sandpaper to finish. Sanding will also remove the mark made in step 2.

6. Mark a line just below the beginning of the taper, and cut the cone free with a wood saw. Sand the bottom of the cone, and then either finish with linseed oil or paint, or simply leave the cone bare and rustic.

22

Page holder

Relieve your thumb of its page-holding duties with this light-hearted yet practical whittled item. Carved with relative ease from a small off-cut of wood, this page holder sits comfortably over the thumb, splaying a book open as it is held in the hand. Once completed you can choose either to sand the wood to a fine finish, or leave your page holder in its rudimentary, functional form.

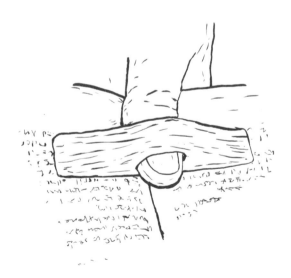

1. Select a piece of wood of approximately 4cm (1½in) diameter and free of any cumbersome knots. Cut a 15cm (6in) length, sawing just below a knot if necessary.

2. Place your knife one-third of the way across the top of the wood and, using a heavy piece of wood to knock the blade down, split the wood in as straight a line as possible.

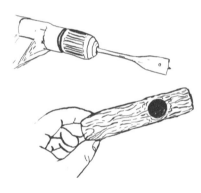

3. Taking the thicker of the two split pieces, lie it on its new flat surface. Selecting a drill bit roughly the same diameter as your thumb, drill a downwards hole one-third of the way in from one end. It is advisable to place scrap wood underneath while drilling, to avoid causing damage to any surfaces.

4. Make a second split cut 1cm (⅜in) behind the first, knocking your penknife down and passing through the hole. This should result in the length becoming a rough rectangular shape.

5. Whittle the shorter side from the hole at an angle down towards the end.

6. Taper the longer end from the hole by using long pull cuts. Whittle this down by repeating the action, until it begins to look the same as the opposite side. Go slowly and carefully; you don't want to cut away more than is necessary.

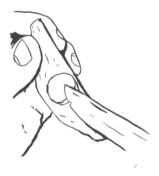

7. Soften the outline of the hole by carefully carving around both sides.

8. Whittle using smaller push cuts to define the shape, before sanding with a medium-grit sandpaper to finish.

23

Hairpin

Surprisingly easy to sculpt, ornate little hairpins like these can also be enormously satisfying to whittle, offering an opportunity to carve using slow, considered strokes. It's best to seek out source material from a particularly sturdy, tough wood. Therefore trees like yew, hornbeam and oak provide the best stems for carving, adding durability to your finished hairpins. As with many of the more delicate carvings in this book, sanding and oiling to finish will embellish your woodwork, highlighting the grain and bringing depth to the wood.

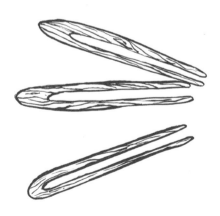

1. Select a 1.5–2cm (⅝–¾in) diameter piece of wood, 15–20cm (6–8in) long. Taper one end, beginning your strokes roughly 7cm (2¾in) back from the top. Do this on both sides to create an even, flat surface around 3mm (⅛in) deep.

2. With a pencil, draw an outline of the hairpin on the flat surface.

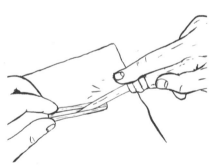

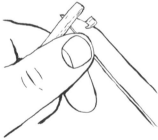

3. Carefully cut the shape out – use a chopping board or equivalent to press down on when necessary. Make sure to leave the bottom part attached to the stick.

4. Carve points on the two ends using small push cuts. Sand the hairpin thoroughly and carefully.

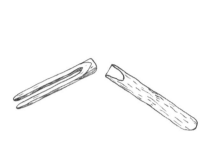

5. Sever the hairpin outline from the rest of the stick – it is no longer necessary as a grip while whittling the hairpin. You can do this either using a wood saw or by whittling down the end of the stick until you have reached the back of the pin.

6. Carve around the bottom outline. Sand the whole hairpin a little more to soften.

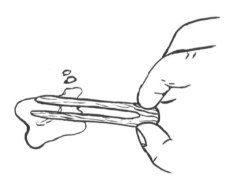

7. Oil the pin to finish (see Helpful Extras, page 17), and leave to one side to dry.

24

Coat hooks

Carving wooden coat hooks is a great example of working alongside the natural characteristics of wood. In crafting these hooks around the join of a branching stem, they will retain the natural strength inherent in the wood, making them durable and less likely to split under pressure or weight. Whittled hooks like these look best in a group, so once you've had a go at making one, continue with the steps to produce a few more before screwing them together onto a length of milled timber. This in turn can then be fixed to a wall or door.

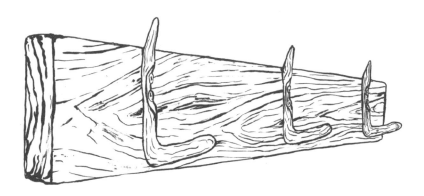

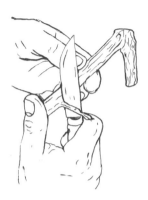

1. Using a saw, cut a branch that features a natural hook like this. Look for where a branch leads out from a main stem, both ideally just over 1cm (⅜in) in diameter.

2. Clean off the side shoots with your penknife. You may wish to wear a thumb guard if using paring cuts.

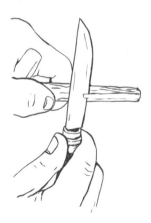

3. Remove the bark entirely.

4. Round the point where the stems meet, shaping it into a smooth ball at the end.

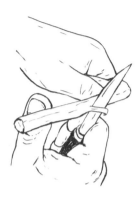

5. Create a flat surface on the opposite side from the hook, using a handful of strokes to get it flat and even.

6. Round both ends of the hook in a similar way to the join in step 4.

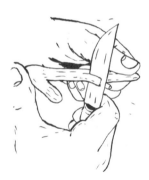

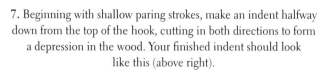

7. Beginning with shallow paring strokes, make an indent halfway down from the top of the hook, cutting in both directions to form a depression in the wood. Your finished indent should look like this (above right).

8. Carve a slope at the top, leaning away from the flat surface made in step 5 – this will form a second hook at the top of the wood. Once completed, taper the edges inwards at the side.

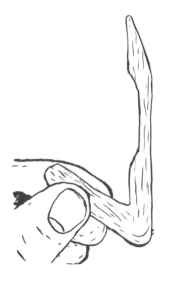

9. Your hook should now look like this. Drill two holes inside the indent so that the hook can be screwed onto a length of board, along with two or three more completed hooks.

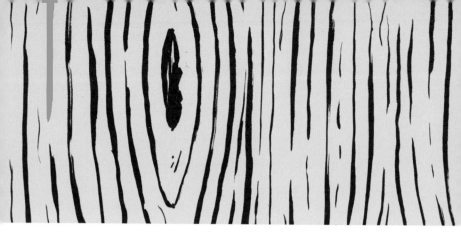

Cork Creations

Often the simplest creations are the most satisfying to make, especially those that recycle material that might otherwise be thrown away. As a medium for carving, cork is fantastically malleable, and is as versatile as it is easy to source. This chapter demonstrates some of the ways corks can be fashioned into useful or decorative objects using a penknife. If bottle corks are in short supply, they can be purchased from online craft suppliers, or obtained as recycled material.

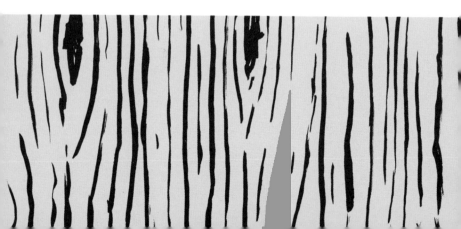

25

Place card holder

Transform 'used' into 'useful' in a few quick steps, repurposing old wine corks into holders for place cards. Whether it is an intimate dinner or a full-blown wedding party, a quick whittle with your penknife will provide ideal decorative stands. These altered corks are also a great way to display photographs around the house, or to store business cards on a desk.

1. Create a flat surface for the cork to sit on by standing it upright and slicing off a straight sliver down one side.

2. With the cork sat on its new flat side, make a cut roughly 1cm (⅜in) deep along its length, just off-centre. Make sure not to cut right through the cork, while ensuring that it is deep enough to hold a card firmly.

Sarah

26

Earphones spool

Untangling earphone cables is one of the most infuriating tasks of the 21st century. Freeing the miniature speakers from a jumble of cords can take up valuable listening time, especially when on the move. Here's a great way of using your penknife to fashion a cork into a convenient spool, keeping your earphones neatly wound and tangle-free inside your pocket.

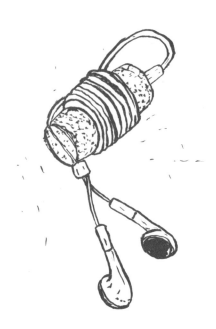

1. Stand the cork upright and cut downwards to a depth of roughly 1cm (⅜in). This will be the slot in which to fasten the two earplugs.

2. At the other end of the cork, mark a shallow 'X' shape across the top.

3. Push a hole through the centre of the 'X' using a pencil. This will create a hole into which you can fit the headphone jack.

27

Succulent pot

With a steady rise in the popularity of miniature houseplants, succulents such as sempervivums, sedums and cacti have been thrust back into the limelight. Displayed in a variety of containers including pots, beakers and glass terrariums, these drought-tolerant plants have become a fashionable way to bring the outside indoors. Whittling a cork into a planting vessel is another great way to exhibit succulents. The porous nature of cork means that it will remain damp after wetting, creating an environment well suited to a growing plant, particularly those with a shallow root system. Follow these simple steps to create an eye-catching container for a slow-growing succulent or even a germinating seed.

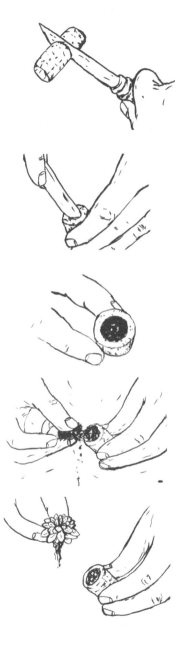

1. Select a dampish cork that has not yet dried out. You can tell if a cork is dry because it will be too brittle to cut cleanly. Place the cork on its side and roll-cut the bottom half away, leaving a length roughly 3–4cm (1¼–1½in) long.

2. Holding the cut cork upright, place your penknife on top at the centre and twist gently. This will cut a small section from the top of the cork. Repeat this action, placing the knife deeper into the crater.

3. Slowly excavate more of the cork, creating a hole at least 2–2.5cm (¾–1in) deep.

4. Fill the hole with light potting compost, e.g. John Innes No.2.

5. Place the succulent or seedling inside the hole and gently firm the soil around the roots.

28

Cork stamp

Cork is a great material for making decorative stamps.
The ease with which it can be carved and its semi-absorbency
makes cork an ideal medium to craft into stamps. There's no
limit to how elaborate or detailed a cork sculpture can be, and
there are many techniques that will achieve impressive results.
Here's a straightforward example however, demonstrating
a simple stamp project to get started with.

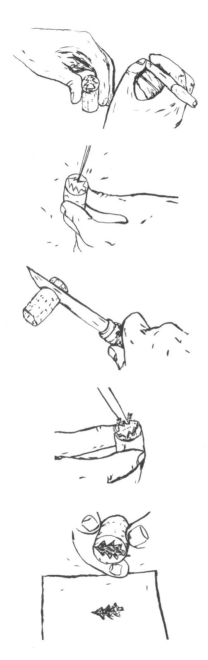

1. Stand the cork upright and draw the outline of a tree on the end with a pen.

2. Use the tip of your penknife to trace carefully along the tree outline, cutting down into the cork to a depth of about 0.5cm (¼in).

3. Placing the cork on its side, cut around the circumference, 0.5cm (¼in) down from the top, where the tree outline is. Make sure that you do not cut right through the cork and that you leave the centre intact – it is important that you do not cut the connection between the tree and the rest of the cork.

4. Using your knife, gently remove the loose cork debris around your tree shape.

5. Your stamp is now ready to be used. You can experiment with different kinds of paint, and ink pads tend to work quite well. Press the stamp down firmly to absorb the colour before printing onto paper or card.

29

Cork stars

Old corks make a great source of carving material and are cheap and easy to get hold of. Here is a way to create miniature stars that can be hung from a wooden mobile. The design for the mobile can be found on page 91. Once painted and dry, you can drill a tiny hole at the top of each star using a small drill bit (1mm). This will create a hole that can be used to string thread for hanging these stars onto the mobile.

1. Stand the cork upright and draw the outline of a star on the end using a pen. The points of the star should reach the sides of the cork.

2. Use the tip of your penknife to carefully cut along the outline, cutting down into the cork about 0.5cm (¼in) deep.

3. Place the cork on its side. Cut around the circumference of the cork, 0.5cm (¼in) down from the top. Unlike the Tree stamp project on page 86, cut right through the cork to separate the star. This is best done by rolling the cork with your knife to cut through it. Your stars can then be painted to finish.

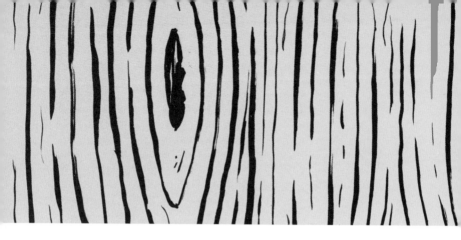

Ornamental Carving

Although many of the projects in this book demonstrate the carving of simple or functional objects, the items featured in this chapter exhibit some of the more ornate applications of a penknife. From attractive accessories like rings, brooches and pendants, to decorative ornaments such as a miniature boat or a flower in bloom, this series of items aims to instil a little artistry into your handiwork. Go slowly when whittling these objects, taking the time to enjoy the process as they gradually begin to take shape.

30

Star mobile

There are many forms of mobile frame, and an even wider variety of objects that can be hung from them. However, the frame shown here can be constructed using only your penknife, a handful of young tree stems and a short length of string. Using clever cuts in place of glue or binding, this simple design allows the knife to do all the work. Birch or hazel are good choices of wood to use, particularly hazel for its young, whippy long stems. Once you've completed your mobile, see Cork stars on page 88 for a guide to carving decorative items to hang from it.

1. Cut three 18–20cm (7–8in) lengths of straight stems, each 1cm (⅜in) in diameter.

2. Taking one of the lengths, use a paring cut to make a 2cm (¾in) slit at one end. It may be advisable to wear a thumb guard while making this cut.

3. At the opposite end of the stick, use push cuts to flatten the last 1.5cm (⅝in) of the end. Make sure that these cuts are made in the same alignment as the slit at the other end.

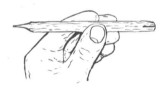

4. Turn the stick over and do the same on the other side. The profile of the stick should now look like this.

5. Many young, small-diameter sticks like these will contain pith at their centre. If this is the case for the material you're using, remove the pith inside the fork of the stick. Once the pith is removed, repeat steps 2–5 for the other two sticks.

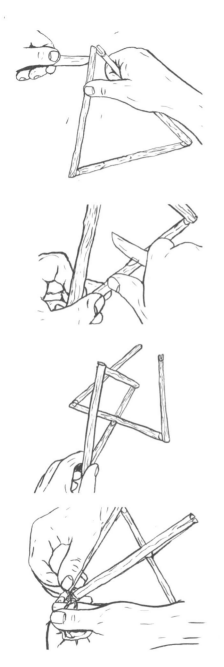

6. Taking all three sticks, fix them together by placing the forked ends inside the slit ends. Place the tip of your knife in the slits and twist to open them so that you can slot in the forks. Neaten up the joins by trimming off any pieces of fork that protrude out from the slits.

7. Holding the joined up triangle upright, carefully pare a 1cm (⅜in) long groove at the centre of the bottom side of the triangle, on the inside. Cut in both directions so that you end up with a little indent in the wood.

8. Repeat steps 1–6 to make a second triangle with sticks 1cm (⅜in) longer. Leave the last connection unmade so that you can place this triangle inside the first. Make a matching indent at the centre of the bottom side of the second triangle, but this time on the outside, so that the indents on both triangles will connect.

9. Join up the last fork and slit, and then line up the apex of the second triangle above the apex of the first triangle. Tie together at the top with string, leaving enough after the knot to hang the mobile. You can now attach the Cork stars from page 88, using thread or translucent fishing wire.

31

Boat

This is a great exercise for anyone wanting to hone more intricate whittling skills. While boats of this design may be carved in a variety of sizes, the minute scale demonstrated in this example is perhaps what makes it so satisfying to craft. However, with this in mind, it is advisable to wear a protective glove or thumb guard while whittling, as the cuts will be made at particularly close quarters. As with many of the items in this chapter, the use of sandpaper will add to the decorative finish of your boat, smoothing out its shape and removing obvious cut marks.

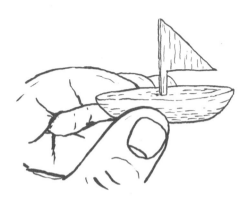

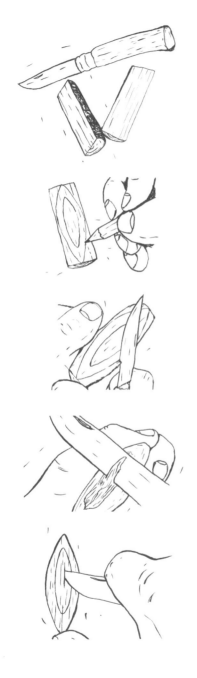

1. Taking a piece of seasoned wood roughly 7cm (2¾in) in length and 2.5–3cm (1–1¼in) in diameter, split it down the middle using a split cut. Place one of the split halves aside.

2. Draw the outline of the inside and outside of a boat on the flat surface of the other split half, as shown. Allow the outer lines to touch the edges of the wood, as this will make it simpler to carve.

3. Whittle around the outer pen marks, carving a slope at each end so that the wood adopts the three-dimensional shape of a boat.

4. Turn the boat over and carve the bottom into a flat surface so that the boat will sit flat.

5. Use the tip of your knife blade to score a line carefully down the middle of the boat, keeping it inside the inner pen marks. Repeat this score several times to make it a few millimetres deep.

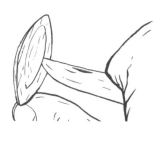

6. Score around the inner pen marks, angling your blade towards the central score line made in step 5. Repeat this action to deepen the cuts. Go slowly, using controlled cuts, to avoid the knife slipping. Still with the tip of your knife, lift the cuts to create a shallow indent for the inside of the boat.

7. Drill a small hole in the middle of your boat and sand down the indent made in steps 5 and 6, using a medium-grit sandpaper.

8. For the sail, take the other half of the split wood from step 1. Cut a thin sliver using a split cut, approximately 2–3mm (⅛in) in depth.

9. Draw the outline of a sail on both sides of the thin piece of wood, drawing the sail pole in the same direction as the wood grain.

10. Carefully carve out the sail shape and taper the pole into a point at the bottom. Finish by sanding rigorously with a fine-grit sandpaper, and then insert the sail firmly into the hole.

32

Brooch and pin

Wooden brooches are a modest but creative example of hand carving that make great gifts or bespoke accessories. The illustrations seen here demonstrate a method of turning a small section of tree branch into a truly decorative item. The joy of making these kinds of brooches is that there is no limit to the shapes and styles you can create. Different trees will vary in colour and grain texture, while different branches will offer individual shapes to work with. When the limbs of trees have had to twist at an angle to reach for sunlight, their wood often takes on a new shape (known as reaction wood), to create extra support with which to combat gravity. So it's worth experimenting with a range of carving material. Birch or hazel are also great carving woods for whittling the pin.

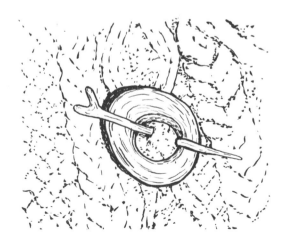

1. To make the pin, get hold of a thin, forked twig roughly 0.5cm (¼in) in diameter. The drier the better for this item, as green wood will be harder to sand smooth at the end. Remove the fork shoots, leaving a length of about 10cm (4in) with a little 'Y' at the top.

2. Remove all the bark, using push cuts for the tricky bits, and whittle down the twig, tapering it at the end.

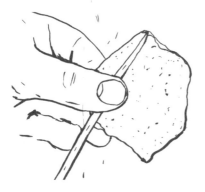

3. Using a medium-grit and then a fine-grit sandpaper, sand the pin so that it is smooth and of a similar diameter throughout.

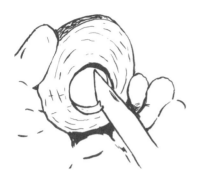

4. For the brooch, refer to the Curtain rings project on page 64. Repeat steps 1–3, except that this time in step 3, saw a thinner slice of wood, roughly 0.5cm (¼in) deep. Whittle the edges down to make them round.

5. Whittle the edges down further to make the wood smoother and more rounded.

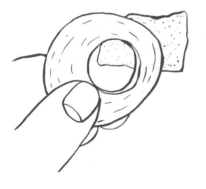

6. Sand the final shape with a medium-grit and then a fine-grit sandpaper, before oiling with linseed to finish.

33

Flower

Turning wooden off-cuts into dazzling flowers has been a
tradition among green woodworkers for decades. Nothing
transforms a short length of hardwood more impressively than
this enjoyable process, revealing a surprisingly ornate creation
from otherwise discarded timber. Trees such as chestnut or
hazel often supply the ideal material for this exercise, offering
wood that is straight and soft to carve, both seasoned and in the
green. While hand-carved flowers like these can be coloured
with paint, their natural state remains equally as attractive.

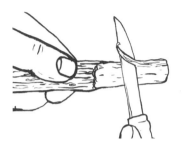

1. Remove the bark from one end of a 30–40cm (12–16in) stick using your penknife blade. Use short push cuts to round the end.

2. Placing your knife 4–5cm (1½–2in) back from the rounded end, make a long push cut down towards it, keeping your blade edge tilted slightly upwards as it travels so that the cut remains shallow. Stop 1cm (⅜in) or so before the end and curl it back by twisting your penknife.

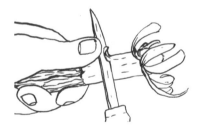

3. Repeat step 2, making cuts all the way around the stick.

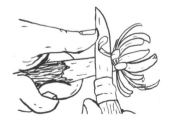

4. Once you've completed a full circle of push cuts, place your knife slightly down from the previous starting position and make a second round of cuts.

5. Repeat rounds of increasingly shorter cuts, resulting in the stick tapering towards the curled shavings. Stop carving at the point when the shavings are only just about joined to the stick.

6. Turn the stick around and carefully make a hole in the bottom with the tip of your penknife.

7. You can now break the flower section away from the rest of the stick – it should snap easily.

8. Find a straight, thin twig of around 20–30cm (8–12in) in length. Whittle one end to a narrow, sharp point.

9. Insert the twig into the hole made in step 6 to complete your flower.

34

Ring

Of all the items in this ornamental chapter, the handcrafted ring is perhaps the most attractive and, once perfected, certainly the most pleasing to accomplish. Carving wooden rings with a penknife requires a great deal of patience, particularly in the initial stages when whittling the basic circular profile. However, the finished item will be more than reward for the time spent carefully crafting it. Selecting the wood for your rings is another enjoyable aspect. Choose a heavyweight hardwood with a fine, tight grain, ideally exhibiting an interesting colouration, such as walnut, cherry or oak. Green wood will shrink as it dries, so it is always best to carve rings using seasoned material. Rings carved from seasoned wood can also be oiled to finish, before sealing with a fine paste wax (although always check ingredients for potential skin allergens). It is recommended that a thumb guard be worn throughout the carving process, as these rings are whittled predominantly using paring cuts.

1. Begin with a square of wood, roughly 1cm (⅜in) in thickness and 4–5cm (1½–2in) in length and width. Make sure that the grain is running across the flat surface of the wood – there should not be any tree growth rings visible on the surface. Drill a hole at the centre, choosing a drill bit a millimetre smaller in size than the size of the ring you want to make.

2. Slowly whittle off the corners, using shallow cuts at first to soften the edges.

3. Use small paring cuts to reduce the wood shape evenly all around. The shape should begin to look like this.

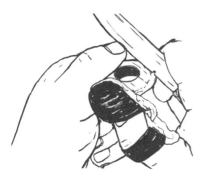

4. To refine the shape further, make slanted cuts to remove the flat edges at the top and bottom, before carving out the middle of the outer circumference. The ring should now be taking on a more distinctive shape.

5. Whittle even closer, making short, careful paring cuts so as not to take off too much wood with each stroke. You now need to sand the inside of the ring thoroughly, so that it is smooth. The sanding process will also widen the hole slightly, so check the fit as you sand. At this stage you can either leave your ring in its more rugged, whittled condition, or sand to a fine finish using progressively finer grit sandpaper.

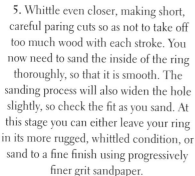

35

Deer

Create a miniature creature of the forest, whittling a variety
of sections that connect to form a deer. Selecting the right
material to carve with is half the fun in this exercise, choosing
a distinctive-looking stem from which to fashion the head.
Adopting the same basic technique, you can also experiment
with different shapes, constructing a host of ornamental
animals. It may be advisable to wear protective gloves when it
comes to the fiddly bits, particularly while making the stop cuts
in steps 2, 8 and 9.

1. Choose a straight branch, approximately 2–3cm (¾–1¼in) in diameter. Cut a section around 5cm (2in) in length.

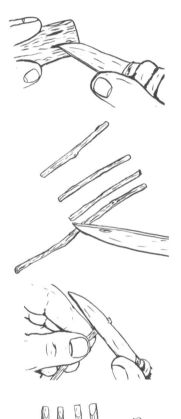

2. Placing the wood on a steady surface and holding it firmly, use the tip of your blade to carefully mark a deep stop cut, creating an indent. Make two of these indents at each end of the wood; these will be the slots into which you'll later fit the deer's legs. A drill can also be used for this step. See Helpful Extras, page 17.

3. For the legs, cut four equally long (roughly 5–6cm/2–2½in), thin stems.

4. Whittle one end of each of the four lengths into a thin wedge shape. Make sure that the wedge tapers to a narrow edge, without it being too long and brittle.

5. You should now have four equal-length stems with wedges at the top. Find a slightly thicker stem and cut wedges at both ends – this will be used as the neckpiece.

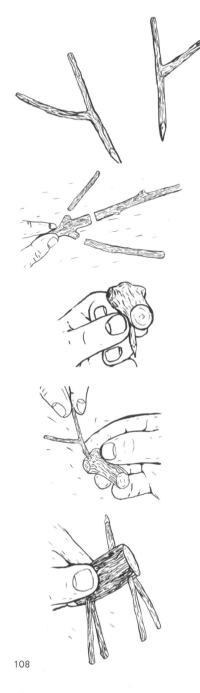

6. Locate two thin, forked twigs and cut them to size, carving wedges at the bottom. These twigs will become the antlers.

7. Locate a branch around 1–2cm (⅜–¾in) in diameter, with two parallel stems leading away at either side. Trim the stems as shown to form the deer's head.

8. Cut the back of the head flat, just before the point where the side stems meet, and make a stop cut underneath it. The neckpiece will slot into this indent. Test the fit, and then remove the neckpiece.

9. Make two stop cuts on the top of the head and fit the antlers inside.

10. Connect up the body with the legs and neckpiece, before completing the deer by adding the head.

36

Pendant

Pendants come in all shapes and sizes, whether gifted as
meaningful gestures or worn casually as fashion accessories.
This project demonstrates the process of whittling a bespoke
pendant from wood, carving the outline of a classic teardrop,
before refining its ornamental profile. The beauty of these
pendants is that they can be carved either in the green or using
seasoned wood; the former will retain the imprints of its lovingly
carved strokes, while the later may be sanded to finish, offering
a smooth surface all around. Seasoned wood may be further
enhanced with a coating of oil, preserving the wood while at
the same time enriching its natural colouration.

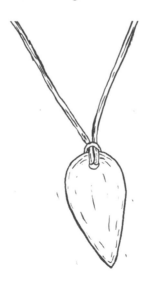

1. Split a small section of wood with a relatively straight grain, placing your knife just off-centre.

2. Placing your knife 0.5cm (¼in) back from the edge, split the larger section again to create a rectangle.

3. Using a pen or pencil, draw the shape of your pendant on one of the flat surfaces of the rectangle.

4. Whittle around the pendant outline, slowly removing the edges of the rectangle by carving away small sections of the wood at a time. A thumb guard will make these paring cuts a little safer to perform. Your pendant should now look like this, with flat surfaces on each side.

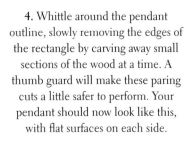

5. Whittle the pendant edges to a point, tapering it on both sides. Once completed, even both pendant faces, making the body thinner.

6. Use the back of your blade to smooth the cut marks and soften the pendant edges. If your penknife has a lockable blade, engage the lock to prevent the blade from closing back into the handle. To finish your pendant, drill a small hole in the top and thread lace through to form the necklace.

37

Bird's egg

Carving a near-perfect, rounded wooden egg can be an enormously satisfying exercise. Attention to detail is key, using precise cuts to form an evenly curved surface. The eggs in this example mimic the natural scale of a songbird egg, such as that of a thrush or blackbird. However, depending on the wood you have available, size is a matter of personal choice, and large eggs can look equally striking. A good way to display the eggs is to place them inside a homemade nest. Nests can be constructed by weaving together sticks or straw, shaping a hollow in the centre. The eggs themselves can also be painted, exhibiting the colours of a chosen species of bird.

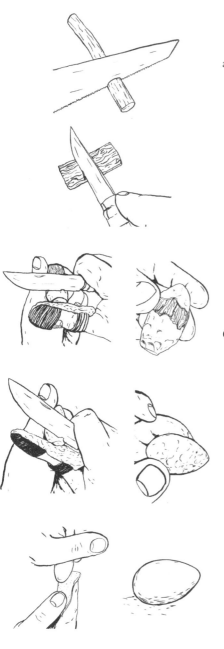

1. Cut a short section of dry wood, around 2–3cm (¾–1¼in) in diameter.

2. Place your penknife blade just off-centre on the stick section, and make a stop cut all the way around, forming a circular line.

3. Use short paring cuts to begin tapering both sides from the line. Make sure you cut equally all around the shape, rounding the ends evenly. Go slowly with this, and you may want to wear a thumb guard or glove for added protection. The shape should now begin to look like this.

4. Whittle down the very ends to a smooth, rounded curve, implementing progressively shorter cuts.

5. Sand thoroughly to finish, beginning with a medium-grit sandpaper before refining with a finer grit.

38

Spinning top

The simplistic shape of this homemade spinning top may appear fairly rudimentary at first, but its modest profile is transformed in motion, coming to life with a flick of the fingers. The enjoyment in carving a functioning spinning top lies in the mastering of its symmetrical shape. While the whittling techniques remain comparatively straightforward, a level of precision is required in order to fashion a balanced and evenly rounded object. The more acutely circular you can carve the two ends, the longer the top will spin. A band of bark is preserved at the lower centre, adding a decorative feature, particularly when the spinning top is rotating.

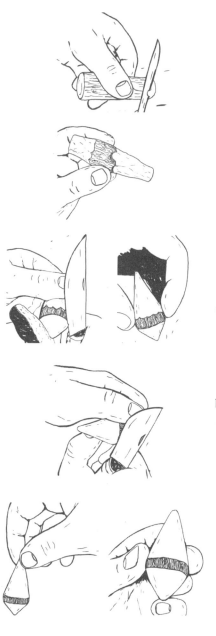

1. Choose a short length of stick with an attractive bark, and taper it at one end using short pull cuts.

2. Carve longer strokes at the opposite end, creating a larger taper than in step 1. Your stick should now look like this.

3. Carve with shorter paring cuts, using a thumb guard for protection. Avoid whittling the bottom to too fine a point – just enough for the spinning top to rotate on. The spinning top should be adopting an evenly rounded shape at both ends now, as shown.

4. Straighten the remaining line of bark with very careful cuts, and even it into a band that remains an equal size all the way around the wood.

5. Test your spinning top by spinning it from your thumb and index finger. Use a flat surface to try it out on. If it falters quickly or does not spin properly after a handful of attempts, the overall shape may still require refining. You can use sandpaper to smooth the shape further.

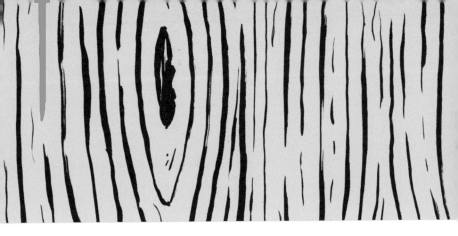

Kitchen Carving

Why limit your whittling to traditional materials? Try your hand at some less conventional carving using fruit and vegetables. A few quick alterations to an onion or cucumber can create a unique table display, while a carrot can be fashioned into a musical marvel. Remember to clean your penknife thoroughly before use in the kitchen, especially when carving items for eventual consumption. It is equally important to clean your knife after use, so as to avoid sticky vegetable residue remaining on the blade.

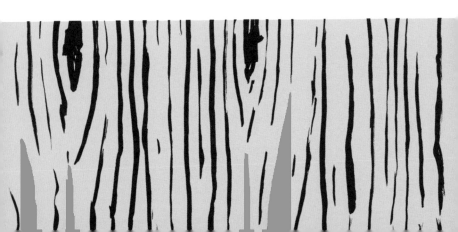

39

Carrot flute

A carrot may not seem to be an obvious choice of musical instrument but it can certainly whistle a tune. That is, of course, after some careful whittling with a sharp penknife. Of the culinary creations listed in this chapter, the carrot flute is perhaps the trickiest to master. In this instance perseverance, as well as practice, makes perfect, and you may be surprised at the results. As with all whittling projects, a well-sharpened blade will deliver the most accurate results. This is perhaps even more the case when carving a vegetable, given the fragility that is produced by a high water content.

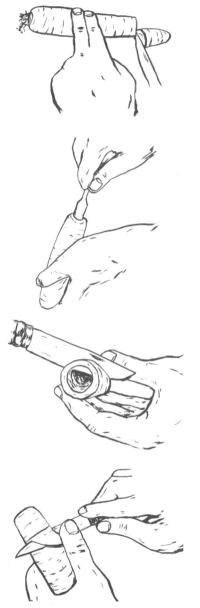

1. Take a good-sized carrot and chop 2.5cm (1in) off the bottom (tapered) end. Put this to one side.

2. Using a drill bit that is just smaller in size than the diameter of your carrot (see Helpful Extras, page 17), drill out the centre by hand. Go slowly with this, and make sure to stop excavations before you reach the other end of the carrot. Alternatively, this can be achieved using your penknife blade, but it will require the use of a slightly shorter carrot. Wash the carrot under a tap when finished.

3. Place your knife 2.5cm (1in) back from the cut end, on the side that will form the front of the flute, and slice down into the cavity. Do not exceed 1cm (⅜in). Looking through the hole, the blade should come down just over one-third of the way into the cavity.

4. Using a push cut 2.5cm (1in) back from the slice made in step 3, make an angled cut downwards, removing a wedge from the carrot and exposing the cavity.

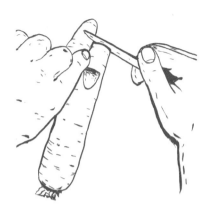

5. Now take the original tip of your carrot. Measure it against the front section of the main carrot (from the end to the slice made in step 3) and trim it to the same size. This piece is going to be placed inside the top hole of the carrot and stop where it meets the slice.

6. Whittle down the trimmed tip so that it slots snugly inside the top cavity of the carrot. Be careful not to push it so far in that you can't take it out again, but do make sure that it will be a tight fit. Once you're happy with the fit, cut away a straight, thin wedge at the top of the tip. The tip can then be pushed back in. The carrot should now produce a whistle when you blow through it.

7. Using a regular 3–5mm drill bit, create evenly spaced holes along the carrot down into the cavity. These will act like the holes on a recorder, changing the pitch of the flute when covered by a finger. You may need to experiment with the spacing of these holes in order to set the pitch right.

40

Apple spiral

An apple spiral produces an eye-catching decoration as simple in design as it is enjoyable to create. Whether forming the centrepiece for a table or adding ornament to your dessert, here's a neat twist on the presentation of an apple.

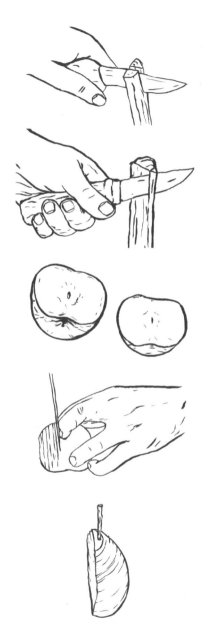

1. Using a split cut, halve and then quarter a straight stick of wood roughly 6cm (2½in) in length.

2. Placing your penknife on a corner of the exposed wood, split off a 2–3mm (⅛in) splinter from the stick, making a 'toothpick' shape. Put to one side.

3. Cut an apple in half, just off-centre, so that one side contains the core and the other does not. Discard the half containing the core.

4. Placing the coreless apple section face down, slice a 1cm (⅜in) wedge from the outer edge on both sides and discard these.

5. Slice the remaining apple into thin, 0.5cm (¼in) strips. Upend the sliced apple, and push your toothpick splinter down through the middle. Twist and splay out the apple slices to form a spiral.

41

Apple candle

Bring a fruity twist to the table with this quick alteration
of an apple. Once your apple has been hollowed out,
the compact shape of regular household tea light candles
is ideal for concealing inside, creating an illuminating
yet ephemeral display.

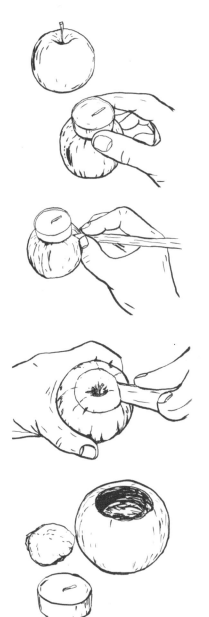

1. Chose a good-sized apple. Remove the stalk and place a tea light on top.

2. Mark around the tea light with a pencil.

3. Put the tea light to one side and cut around the marked circumference with your penknife.

4. Excavate the hole carefully, cutting downwards at the sides so that the tea light sits snugly when placed inside.

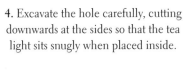

42

Cucumber chain

In my book, there's only one way to decoratively prepare a cucumber. Being juicy and light, the fleshy centre is easily removed, making it simple to hollow out and slice. Produced using a handful of quick cuts, rings of cucumber are then craftily connected to form the illusion of an interlocking chain.

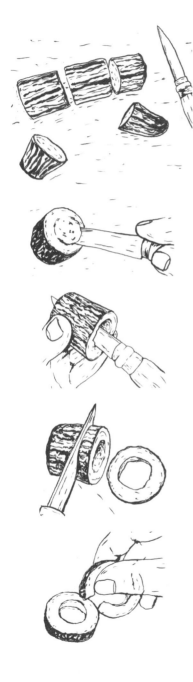

1. Slice the cucumber into chunks of roughly the same diameter and discard the ends.

2. Make a cut into the first cucumber chunk at an angle towards the middle, 0.5cm (¼in) from the outer edge. Slowly rotate the cucumber in your other hand so that the knife cuts smoothly in a circle, removing a cone from the centre. Repeat this action at the other end of the cucumber chunk.

3. Push your knife right through the centre of the cucumber. Take it out, turn the blade 90 degrees and repeat the action. This will result in an 'X' being cut through the middle of the cucumber. Now carefully scrape out the centre, keeping the same diameter hole as at the front and back.

4. Repeat steps 2 and 3 with each of the remaining cucumber sections, and then slice them all into rings of approximately 1cm (⅜in) thickness.

5. Taking a cucumber slice, make a cut through the ring edge. Open the ring at the cut and push another ring through the gap. Repeat this process to form a chain.

43

Onion flower

Get crafty in the kitchen with this quick culinary carving. By
making use of the rings inside an onion, you can transform its
simple shape into the petals of a blooming flower.

1. Cut a red onion in half across the middle. Taking the bottom half, remove the papery outer skin.

2. Holding the half onion in one hand, place your penknife across the top surface so that the knife point stops at the centre, and cut down 1cm (⅜in) deep.

3. Cut down with the knife so that the tip of the blade lifts upwards while the rest of the blade cuts downwards. Stop the knife short before it cuts right through the bottom root section of the onion. Repeat step 3 three more times to make the shape of a cross on the top of the onion.

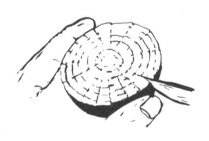

4. Use the same method to divide each of the four segments into two. This step can then be repeated once more to give 16 segments. Once cut, open up the sections carefully using your thumb, allowing the flower to come to life.

44

Peacock tail

This is perhaps one of the quickest of the kitchen carving projects, but it is also one of the most ornate. Given the stark contrast between the colour (as well as texture) of the flesh and the skin of a courgette, a few quick slices can create surprising effects. With the deep green courgette skin remaining at the tips of the 'feathers', this miniature display is cheerfully reminiscent of a peacock tail. You can also try out the same process using a cucumber or the yellow varieties of courgette.

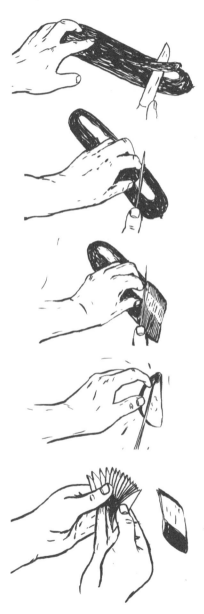

1. Cut a courgette in half lengthways down the middle. Taking one of the halves, remove a thin slice of skin along the top.

2. Slice the half courgette at an inwards angle as shown, and remove the end section.

3. Keeping the same knife angle, cut 14–16 thin slices, each time stopping your knife just before it cuts right through to the bottom.

4. Upending the slices into a stack face down, make a single cut at the angle shown, leaving a crescent shape on the left.

5. Hold the crescent in one hand and, with the other hand, carefully open up the feathers clockwise to display the peacock tail. Make sure you hold the slices tightly together as you do this.

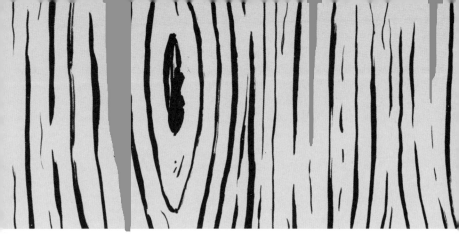

The Natural World

Not every penknife project needs to result in the completion of a carved object. As this chapter illustrates, the versatility of a penknife extends to a range of applications, proving once again how practical it can be. Comprising projects relating to both flora and fauna, this final section once again embraces the wild outdoors. From fashioning a biodegradable bird feeder to the grafting of an apple tree, these activities reconnect the rustic penknife with the wider natural world.

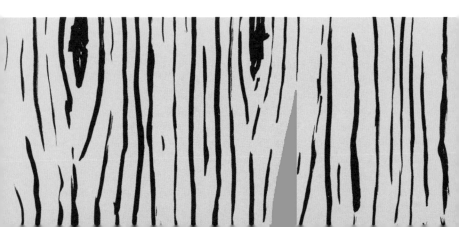

45

Graft an apple tree

Grafting is an age-old horticultural technique whereby a young stem is pruned from a healthy, well-formed tree and attached to the roots of another tree using a small, sharp blade. The advantage of grafting is that it allows you to harness the particular qualities of both plant sections, joining them together to form one tree. When this process is applied to apple trees, the young stem wood (known as a 'scion') will dictate the variety of apple that is produced, while the root section (known as the 'rootstock') will dictate the vigour and size of the eventual tree. It is important that you select the right rootstock to suit your tree's ultimate intended site. More information on apple grafting can be found in Sources, page 143.

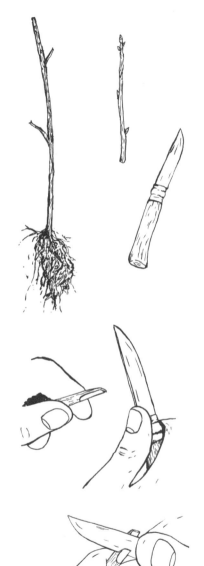

Rootstocks are graded according to the particular tree habit they will produce, ranging widely between dwarfing and vigorous growth, and can be purchased from online retailers. Scion wood can be cut from existing trees, selecting one-year-old stems from your favoured varieties. The stems should be collected in late autumn and stored in a bucket of damp sand until ready to be grafted in spring.

1. Select your rootstock and cut it to size, slicing roughly 30cm (12in) up from the roots. Make the cut below a bud.

2. Cut a slope at the end of the rootstock, forming a thin wedge roughly 2cm (¾in) in length.

3. Now add a small 'tongue', making a short cut back in the opposite direction. Perform this cut from halfway down along the wedge of the previous cut. Press your thumbs together as you do this to avoid the knife slipping. You may wish to wear gloves for this exercise.

6. Join the two pieces together, interlocking the 'tongues'.

7. Wrap a rubber band around the connected stems, covering the join. Paint over the rubber band section with grafting wax. This is available at garden centres and online and helps to prevent infection from getting into the join.

4. Take your scion wood selection and line the stems up against the rootstock one by one. Select a scion stem with a bottom diameter equal to that of the prepared rootstock tip.

5. Holding the scion wood with the cut end uppermost, repeat the same two cuts as for the rootstock in steps 2 and 3, mirroring their size and shape.

8. Prune away the top of the scion wood leaving three or four buds above the graft, and plant it in a compost-filled pot. Keep your young tree in a sheltered spot, watering regularly and protecting it from any frost. Once the tree has begun sprouting strong new shoots, plant it out into well-cultivated soil during the dormant season.

46

Bird feeder

During the colder months of the year, food sources for local birdlife can become less available, particularly in areas experiencing temperatures around and below freezing. Give your resident birdlife a helping hand with an attractive yet ephemeral bird feeder. These feeders are quick to assemble using your penknife, and can be made from a variety of tough-skinned fruits, such as pumpkins, marrows and, as seen here, a squash. Although these feeders will sustain a surprising number of refills, they will eventually begin to rot, at which point they may be disposed of or composted in their entirety.

1. Cut a large squash in half. Use your penknife to scrape out the seeds from inside, leaving an empty hole at the centre.

2. Select or cut a stick that is a little longer than the width of the squash. Create a sharp point at one end using a handful of short pull cuts.

3. Push the stick through the centre of the squash, and then blunt the sharp end of the stick with your penknife. The stick will act as both support for the string and an additional perch for feeding birds.

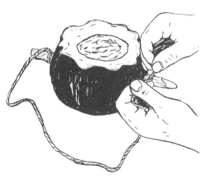

4. Tie a 60–80cm (24–32in) length of string to each end of the stick outside of the squash. Pour a few handfuls of mixed birdseed into the cavity of the squash before hanging it outdoors in a suitable bird-friendly spot.

47

Tap a birch tree

Maple syrup is one of nature's sweetest treasures and the process of extracting the sap has been practised for hundreds of years. Birch trees may also be tapped using the same technique. As with maple, birch sap forms a delicious syrup when boiled but also makes for a refreshing drink in its own right, without the need for refining. Here's a simple method for carving a birch tap from foraged wood. A bucket to collect the sap can then be hung from the spile itself. Do remember that tapping tree species of any kind will leave a wound, exposing them to dangers from pests and disease, so you must have permission from the landowner before you tap a tree. All tap-holes must be plugged immediately after use, allowing the tree to recover.

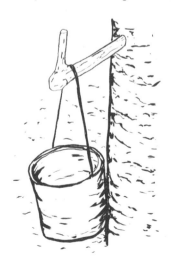

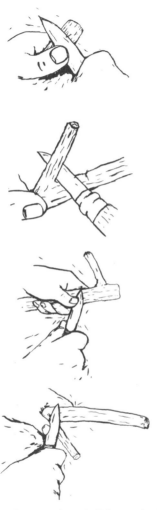

1. Look for a smallish, forked branch to work with. Cut one of the forked ends to around 10–15cm (4–6in) and the other to roughly 5cm (2in). Taking the longer fork, clean off the bark using your blade and then taper it at the end using a series of push cuts.

2. Make a sloping cut leading down towards the tapered end from the point where the forked lengths meet. This will make a smooth channel to help guide the sap.

3. Holding the tapered end of the fork, make an angled push cut downwards to begin a groove at the bottom of the fork.

4. Holding the other end, push cut a similar slope to meet the previous cut and complete the groove. Repeat steps 3 and 4 on the opposite side. These grooves will ensure that the sap will run downwards into the bucket.

You are now ready to drill the trunk of your chosen tree, selecting a spot roughly 1m (1yd) from the ground. The hole will need to be slightly smaller in diameter than your whittled spile, drilled at an angle upwards to a depth of around 5cm (2in). Trees should only be tapped if they're of a girth of 30cm (12in) or more. Gently hammer in the wooden spile using a mallet before hanging your bucket and leaving it to fill slowly.

48

Prepare a fish

This project shows how to prepare or 'clean' a freshly caught river fish (such as a trout or salmon) for cooking. Using only your penknife, these straightforward steps illustrate how to remove and discard unwanted elements such as the entrails, head and the blood sack (a long artery running parallel with the spine). As outlined in step 5, blood from this artery should be squeezed out, as it can otherwise contribute a bitter taste to the meat when cooked. While this exercise may not suit the faint-hearted, it remains an efficient method of preparing a fish, conserving as much of the meat as possible. Always make sure that your fish is killed humanely before cleaning.

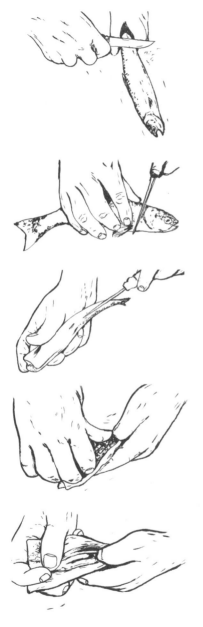

1. Descale the fish by holding it by the tail and scraping the blade of your penknife across the skin. Repeat this action, running from tail to head until most of the scales have been removed.

2. To remove the head, make a single, diagonal cut beginning just behind the gills and finishing in front of the pectoral fin (shown beneath index finger).

3. Having removed the head, place the tip of your knife in the bottom vent hole in front of the tail. Slice upwards in the direction of the (removed) head, opening up the belly of the fish.

4. Remove the entrails by hand. The internal anatomy of river fish isn't overly dense and therefore this step is relatively quick to perform.

5. Run your thumb along the inside of the fish from tail to head, applying pressure to the spine in order to squeeze all the blood from under it. If you prefer, the butt of your penknife handle can be applied in place of the thumb. Once the blood has been squeezed out, cut away the tail and rinse the whole fish in clean water.

49

Taking a cutting

Taking cuttings is a great way to produce your own plants from a particular shrub or tree. Whether you wish to top up the number already in your garden, or a certain variety of plant has caught your eye, a hardwood cutting taken during a plant's dormant period (late autumn through winter) can be made using a few simple strokes with your penknife. While not all plants will reproduce from cuttings, many flowering shrubs will (such as Hydrangea, Forsythia and Philadelphus), often making it a faster and more effective way to propagate than growing from seed. As new roots develop below the soil level, make sure they receive adequate watering, and you should see green shoots appearing in spring.

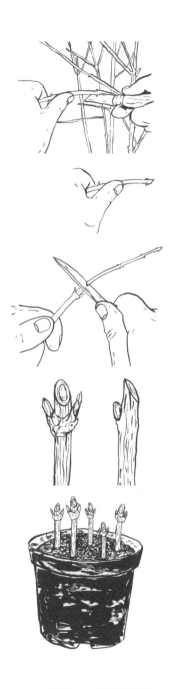

1. Select a healthy looking stem on your chosen shrub. It should be of roughly pencil thickness, and present a handful of healthy buds. Place your knife underneath, below a bud close to the main branch. Holding it tight in your other hand, slice through the stem in one motion.

2. Count three buds up from the bottom cut made in step 1, and use a pull cut to carve a slope above this third set of buds.

3. Refine the slope cut by making a more careful cut closer to the buds. Angle the slope away from the buds, as this will enable water to run off, avoiding damage from rot. This step can also be applied to plants displaying alternate, single buds, as shown.

4. Repeat this process to prepare a handful of cuttings. Fill a pot with compost and firm it down, and then prepare deep holes in which to place your stems. Submerge the stems by two-thirds, so that two sets of buds are beneath the compost.

50

Opening a bottle

Wood carving can be thirsty work, and a cool refreshment from
the fridge often rewards a good day's graft. If you find yourself
without a bottle opener, simply tuck your blade back inside
its handle and let your trusty penknife do the rest.

1. Place one hand around the top of
the bottle neck, gripping it tightly.

2. Hold your penknife in the other
hand with the blade closed and the
butt of the handle facing outwards.

3. Place the metal of the closed knife
blade between your index finger
and the bottle top.

4. Apply pressure with your knifed
hand, twisting the metal upwards
while holding your other hand tight
around the bottle. The bottle top
should come away in one motion.

Sources

Knives

The majority of exercises in this book have been illustrated using pocket knives made by Opinel. While there are many forms and makers of penknife, I prefer Opinel knives for their durability, functional versatility and traditional design. Opinel offer a vast range of different folding knives which can be viewed on their website: www.opinel.com

Opinel knives may be purchased in the UK directly from Whitby & Co. www.whitbyandco.co.uk

Tool/protection suppliers

UK: www.woodsmithexperience.co.uk
US: www.highlandwoodworking.com
Sharpening/whetstones:
www.whitbyandco.co.uk

Associations/organizations
British Wood Carvers Association (BWA)
For links and information on wood carving in the UK visit:
www.britishwoodcarversassociation.co.uk

National Wood Carvers Association (NWCA)
For links and information on wood carving in the US visit: www.chipchats.org

Woodland Trust
For information on tree care and conservation in the UK visit:
www.woodlandtrust.org.uk

Apple grafting

Background and contextual information for the Apple Grafting item in this book has been simplified for the text. For further information regarding aftercare for grafted apple trees as well as the sourcing of appropriate materials, online information is available at: www.rhs.org.uk

Hardwood cuttings

There are many plants that will respond well to propagation through hardwood cutting, and the following list is by no means comprehensive. Further information on hardwood cuttings can be read online at: www.rhs.org.uk

Abelia, Deutzia, Buddleja, Cornus, Forsythia, Philadelphus, Ribes, Viburnam, Berberis, Spiraea, Kerria, Weigela, rose, poplar, willow, Ilex, fig, mulberry and quince.

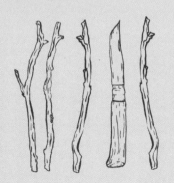

Acknowledgements

I would like to thank the lovely team at Pavilion involved in putting this book together; in particular Katie, Michelle, Caitlin and Katie Hewett. Special thanks to Krissy for her guidance along the way, as well as helpful suggestions relating to the book's structure and content.

Working with Maria Nilsson on this book has been a joy from start to finish. I can't thank her enough for the accuracy, speed and detail with which her beautiful illustrations were delivered. Maria's ability to interpret and re-imagine my often convoluted descriptions has formed the backbone for this project, and I have enjoyed seeing each of the 50 items come to life through her wonderful drawings.

Thanks also to Clemmie and Marie for putting up with the mountain of wood shavings that piled up in our home during the planning of this project!

Lastly I want to thank my dad, who taught me how to gut my first fish.